Understanding Depression

Grahame Cossum

I would like to dedicate this book to my mother who unfortunately passed away as I was writing it. I will be forever grateful for her inspiration and motivation. Thanks, Mum! I miss you!

Contents

Author Bio

Grahame Cossum was born and grew up in Northern Ireland and still lives there today, with his wife, a parrot, numerous chickens and their horses. He is a certified Clinical Hypnotherapist, Neuro-Linguistic Programming Practitioner, Integral Eye Movement Practitioner and lifelong student of the human mind.

He overcame a serious accident and suffered from depression for a decade, before finally managing to overcome it. This experience was partly what motivated him to begin writing and his first two books, *Make Peace with Your Harshest Critic, YOU* and *Focused Awareness* are self-help books that are available through Amazon. Grahame coaches his readers to achieve peace of mind and control in their everyday lives. In this book, *Understanding Depression* Grahame takes you on a personal journey through depression and addresses common misunderstandings about the illness he himself endured.

Grahame hopes that his books will encourage others to overcome their own battles in life and allow them to move on to better, happier and more successful things and fulfilling lives.

Introduction

When I went through ten years of situational/reactive depression following a serious accident several things were exceptionally difficult to come to terms with and which are the inspiration for this book. The first was the lack of honest answers to questions that I had. The amount of ignorance, misunderstanding, myth, fallacy and bad advice surrounding this illness is astounding. These misunderstandings lead to stigma, prejudice, discrimination and potentially social isolation for the sufferer. I intend to address a lot of these in the following chapters and will be giving you insights both from a sufferer's point of view, as the author of two self-help books and from my work as a therapist—now retired. What follows is 101 chapters set out in question and answer format covering the most popular questions I have been asked, and also questions I would have liked answers to on my journey through depression. Accept my apologies if I haven't included one of yours.

Another difficult aspect to come to terms with was other people's reactions when I told them I was suffering from depression. Most times this was met with "what have you got to be depressed about?" or "all you need to do is think positive" or my favorite "just pull yourself together." Have you endured this? These platitudes are covered in depth, and how to deal with them. There's something in here for everyone no matter what stage of the depression journey you are at, especially if you are at the beginning. The book is also invaluable if you know someone going through this illness and want to educate yourself about what they are experiencing.

Depression is not some sort of lifestyle choice or a way of getting attention; it can be a serious life-changing experience for millions of people. Depressed people are confused by the tsunami of conflicting information available. Some people believe depression can be prayed away, exercised away or maybe someone could just snap out of it if they tried hard enough . . . certainly not possible! Worse still, they are told that other people are worse off, and they just need to be grateful. My intention is to explode those myths and misunderstandings for you. This book will give you a deeper understanding of what exactly it is you are going through. Knowledge is power so they say, and I want to equip you to have that power.

There will be a common theme running through the book. It is my firm belief that some form of talk therapy is *essential* to help someone get better and hopefully stay better. I will address the practical aspects of finding a therapist and what to ask them to ensure they are a good fit for you. This is not a therapy book as I don't believe therapy is possible through the medium of a book. There are however loads of hints and tips to help you gain a better understanding of this illness. Depression is such a complicated and individual experience that it needs the therapy to be bespoke, nuanced and as idiosyncratic as the person suffering it. This really needs to be done face-to-face over a period of time and with sensitivity by a professional.

You will notice that I talk about depression as being an illness. I make no apology for calling it so because someone that is suffering from depression can feel and look very ill indeed. In my opinion, calling it a mood disorder trivializes the very real suffering people experience. It is a strange quirk of this illness that everyone seems to have an opinion on it and will quite happily tell you how to get out of it even though they have never been through it themselves. I will separate the fact from the fiction for you. I will also give you some hints and tips on how to deal with these people.

Lastly, I have deliberately kept the chapters short because I know from my own experience with depression that I had the attention span of a gnat, and my memory retention was terrible. For the same reason, each chapter is a separate entity and rarely refers to each other so there is no need to read the book in one or two sittings. You can start at the back and read forward if you like or just dip in and out when you have the motivation that is ever so sadly lacking with depression.

I am hoping by the time you get to the end of this book you will realize you are not alone and there are millions of people going through exactly what you are right now. The illness can be very isolating and insular. It can be a very lonely place to be. It is my sincere wish that my little book triggers you into getting the help you need and deserve and brings you out of that dark place. Let's get started on that journey heading towards the light.

What is the most depressing thing in life?

If you are reading this book, you already know the answer to this question. Suffering depression is the most depressing thing in life. You might look like you are alive, but you are not really living. It's a sort of non-life existence.

I suffered depression myself for ten years. No, that's not completely accurate, *I still suffer from depression.* Maybe not to the same intensity, but it's bad enough that it can make life miserable on a frequent basis. Depression can sometimes feel like you are walking around wearing a lead coat that you are not allowed to take off.

It's not much fun having to look at life through crap-colored goggles, it's not much fun feeling totally alone and isolated in this world although being surrounded by people. It's not much fun knowing the only relief you might get is the few hours you are asleep . . . if you are lucky. For most depressed people sleep does not bring rest and recuperation. It can make them feel more exhausted than when they went to bed

It's not much fun listening to people telling you to snap out of it, think positive, listen to music or go for long walks when all you want to do is go to sleep and never wake up again. What we crave is understanding, not platitude or pep talks. We absolutely know that in your mind you are thinking you are being helpful when in reality you are making the situation considerably worse. We have tried all of those things and they all have something in common, they do not work.

But, worse than all those things put together is the knowledge that it's going to happen again tomorrow and the next day . . . and the next and the next. What's really scary is the fact you know you have no options, no alternative, other than having to face this tsunami of emotion which ranges from indifference and numbness to internal self-hatred and sometimes blind fury. Where for *some* people even death can seem like an attractive alternative to life. We are not warriors fighting some sort of heroic battle. Our shield is battered, and our sword is broken but we have to carry on.

So spare a thought when someone tells you they are suffering depression and they have a smile on their face. You have no comprehension of the depths the human mind can sink to when in the grip of the invisible monster we call depression. And if you have been given this book so you might obtain a better understanding of the illness count yourself very lucky indeed that the individual that gave it to you felt safe enough to trust you with their innermost darkest secret. Believe me, for them it was excruciatingly difficult.

A smile can hide a universe of pain and suffering. A socially acceptable mask helps us to function in the real world. It's something we hide behind to avoid the stigma, prejudice, discrimination and possible social isolation this illness can bring. We absolutely want to be happy, but we seem to have lost the ability. That's our life.

What is depression?

Everyone experiences times when they feel low. Breakups, job losses, bereavement, accidents, pain and disappointment are only a few of the hundreds of thousands of reasons someone can feel a bit down—it's the price of admission for being a member of the human race. But these feelings naturally pass. If these feelings last a long time, keep coming back or are interfering with your life, it could be a sign of depression. Depression is an illness. People that are suffering from it look ill and they feel ill. I certainly did when I had it. I always have been of the opinion that calling it a mood disorder somehow trivialized the very real suffering someone goes through.

Depression is an extremely complex and multifaceted condition and its causes are not 100% fully understood. There are however factors that have the potential to lead to depression.

Genetics passed down through generations can play a part in the onset of depression. Did members of your family suffer from depression?

Long-term physical illness can lead to depression. Heart disease and cancer are only two of thousands of ailments associated with the illness. A long-term physical illness can cause a person to lose hope for the future and feel helpless in the face of something they feel they have no control over.

Pain and depression are very well documented. Chronic pain with no chance of a resolution can be very difficult to live with as it can be non-relenting and pervasive. I can personally testify to its effects as I have lived with chronic pain for over thirty years.

Psycho/social factors. This can go right back to childhood. Any form of sexual, emotional or physical abuse in the early years can trigger depression in adulthood, as can divorce or the death of a parent.

A life-changing event. Even one supposedly as joyous as pregnancy and or the birth of a child can have a dramatic effect on someone's psyche. Postpartum depression is a lot more common than we think as most of it probably goes undiagnosed.

Medication, recreational drugs and alcohol. Depression can be a side effect of a lot of different medications—even anti-depressants—believe it or not. If you are feeling depressed after starting any sort of medication, check with the pharmacist. If they can't help you, an appointment with your doctor might be in order.

There is a well-documented correlation between the use of recreational drugs and or excessive alcohol and depression. If you are using either or both and suffering depression this normally requires a professional multidisciplinary approach to treatment. I have listed only a few of the possible causes of depression so I apologize if I have not included yours.

Different types of depression

Probably the biggest misunderstanding you will encounter from other people about depression is that they think it is all the same and it is suffered exactly the same way by everyone. If you heard the word *depression* ten years ago it probably would have triggered images of someone with a serious mental health issue. Today, the word depression has become nearly meaningless thanks to social media. It seems now you can be *depressed* if your favorite television show is coming to an end or because Mom took away your games machine. This list contains the most common types of depression. Each of these types would require a book of their own to do them justice. I strongly encourage you to do some research of your own on each of them because knowledge is power, and you need the knowledge to know what you are dealing with. Now, when you open up to someone and they say, *"Oh, I was depressed once and just snapped out of it"* you will be able to say, *"Really, which type of depression did you have?"*

- **Major depression:** Can also go by the names clinical depression, major depressive disorder or unipolar depression.

- **Dysthymia:** Also known as persistent depressive disorder and/or high-functioning depression.

- **Postpartum depression:** Also known as peripartum depression.

- **Seasonal affective disorder:** Or (SAD) for short.

- **Bipolar disorder:** Also known as manic depression.

- **Psychotic depression.**

- **Premenstrual dysphoric disorder:** Also known as PMDD.

- **Atypical depression.**

- **Disruptive mood dysregulation disorder:** Also known as DMDD.

- **Situational depression:** Also known as adjustment disorder and/or reactive depression.

Another common misunderstanding surrounding depression is that some people think that it has to be triggered by an event to come into their lives. Even a quick bit of research of the above depressions will reveal that isn't the case at all. It's probably why the most common sentence a depressed person hears from other people is *"what have you got to be depressed about?"*—usually said in either a condescending or judgmental tone. Even the depressed person themselves can be confused if they don't know the different types of depression. It's very common for them to say, "I am extremely depressed, but don't know why?" They too think that something needs to have happened in their lives to cause this.

All of the above types of depression have one factor in common; they should be taken *very* seriously. If you have been consistently suffering five or more symptoms from the *symptoms of depression* chapter, I would strongly urge you to make an appointment with your doctor for an assessment as soon as possible. It doesn't necessarily mean you have depression as several physical ailments can mimic the illness.

Symptoms of depression

I have listed some of the more common and not so common symptoms of depression; hopefully, it will give you a clearer understanding of what it actually is and what to look out for.

Trouble concentrating, remembering details and making decisions. Depression seems to have the ability to shut down those parts of the brain that help us think straight. Concentrating for long periods of time can seem like an endurance test and reading, an impossible chore. Short-term memory can be affected making concentration an even more frustrating task than it already is. An inability to make decisions can be a difficult symptom to live with especially if you are one of those people that decision-making came easily to. In extreme cases of depression, a person can even have difficulty deciding whether to have a shower or brush their teeth, with all the obvious problems that can bring along.

Fatigue. There can be no doubt that the daily battle with depression can be an exhausting experience. The illness can be all-consuming and takes up a tremendous amount of real estate in the mind. This battle can cause the sufferer to want to sleep more than normal, but this sleep is seldom restorative. Sleeping during the day can upset the natural rhythm of our body clock and make normal sleeping patterns problematic which in turn can cause even more fatigue.

Guilt, worthlessness and helplessness. Do you ruminate constantly about something you did or failed to do in the past? Does this rumination trigger feelings of "if only things had been different?" Do the words "I should/shouldn't have" feature largely in your internal conversation? Do you feel constantly worthless and feel you have no purpose or meaning to your life, and also feel you are powerless to do anything about it? That no one can help you, or you are beyond help and a burden?

Sleep problems. Do you wake up more tired than when you went to bed? Depression is well documented as causing sleep disturbance and insomnia. In an attempt to make up for lost sleep at night do you sleep during the day? This can upset the body's natural rhythm and make natural restorative sleep difficult to obtain. It can very easily lead to a vicious circle of sleep deprivation and/or the need for excessive sleep.

Pessimism and hopelessness. Do you feel that as far as you are concerned every silver lining has a cloud? Can you turn a positive experience into a negative one in the blink of an eye? Do you see the negative side of everything and feel helpless and powerless to affect change in your life? Have you given up hope of ever overcoming your depression?

Crankiness. Do you seem to have a short fuse and snap at those who love and care for you, and then you are consumed by guilt for your behavior? Do you have persistent feelings of self-hate that you project onto other people by lashing out at the slightest hint of criticism? On the opposite side of this do you have an all-consuming feeling of sadness and loss more akin to grief that causes you to be tearful a lot of the time?

Symptoms (Part 2)

Loss of interest. Have you lost interest in things you once found very interesting for instance hobbies, your job and even people? Do you feel it's not worth the effort to keep a relationship going? Has your libido been affected so much that you have lost interest in being intimate? Do you deliberately isolate yourself away from other people because you can't bear the thought of having to pretend you are fine?

Overeating or loss of appetite. When I went through my ten years of depression, I gained 60 lbs. and what's more, I didn't care. What's your relationship with food like? Do you overeat to try and fill an emotional void that can't be filled or maybe you do the opposite and restrict your food intake as a way of punishing yourself or feeling in control?

Persistent feelings of emptiness. When I was in the depths of depression myself, I remember hearing a line from a Neil Diamond song that I think sums up the void that depicts depression perfectly: "I've got an emptiness deep inside and I've tried but it won't let me go." Do you feel that emptiness? What have you tried to fill that void with? Food, alcohol, drugs, gambling, shopping or maybe even *all* of the above. All five of these have one thing in common, they are a short-term solution to a long-term problem and can create even bigger problems like addiction. They will *never* work long term.

All of the above are well-known symptoms of depression, now I would like to add a few of my own gleaned from my personal experience. They can be overlooked sometimes but are significant.

Anger, resentment and bitterness. Are you angry at the world in general or do you blame someone or something in particular for your predicament? Do you find yourself holding grudges and saying words like "life's not fair," "what did I do to deserve this?" "why me?" Do you loathe the person you have become and ruminate constantly about how things "used to be?"

What's the point? Do you feel there is no point to your life and that there is no point in even trying to get better as it is doomed to failure? Is your personal hygiene suffering because you don't see the point in having a shower or brushing your teeth even though you know it might make you feel a little bit better?

Do other people comment that you seem depressed? It's a strange phenomenon of depression that sometimes other people can spot depression in us before we recognize it ourselves. We can very easily push those feelings to the one side by rationalizing that we have *just been working too hard* or maybe we are a bit under the weather. It can take quite a while and a few comments from other people before the penny finally drops.

A little word of warning. Most people looking at this list will be thinking "I have experienced most of those symptoms at different times in my life." But that is not depression; it's simply the ups and downs of life. Depression is when these symptoms persist for weeks and maybe months on end with no let up, and no matter what you do you can't seem to shake them off. This should be enough of a red flag to trigger making an appointment with your doctor, if you are reading this book, taking online depression tests and hanging out in online forums asking questions about the illness—it might be time to take some action and consult a professional.

Lastly, you don't need to be experiencing *all* of the symptoms to get a diagnosis of depression. For instance, I personally never suffered any sleeping problems for the ten years I went through it. I also never suffered any problems with concentration and or short-term memory loss.

Depression is an extremely complex and unique experience for the individual going through it. It can require professional help to unravel this conundrum and come up with a tailor-made treatment plan specific to you. The sooner you start the process the better. Depression rarely gets better with a *wait and see* approach.

Isn't depression just sadness?

Comparing depression to sadness is like comparing getting hit with a bus to falling off your bike—they both hurt but the severity of the event is what matters. Yes, of course there is an element of feeling sad because of depression, but it's far from being the complete story. The illness is too multifaceted and complex to be pigeon-holed or reduced to one particular symptom.

Generally, sadness does not require therapy and or medication to overcome, with the possible exception of extreme grief. Depression frequently requires *both* these interventions. What is not commonly known is that depression can share a few of the characteristics of grief. Some people can quite literally feel they are mourning the death of the person they once were; they mourn that aspect of the self they feel will never return and be lost forever.

I think the misunderstanding of comparing depression to sadness can trace its roots right back to people that have never suffered the illness. They mistakenly compare their experience of sadness or feeling down with a complex mental health issue in the belief they are the same. They are in effect comparing apples to oranges without ever having tasted an orange.

This mindset can result in the sufferer feeling stigmatized as they are thought of as *just feeling sad* rather than someone who is enduring very real suffering for potentially a very long time. Unfortunately, some people use the platitude of *just sad* to trivialize and dismiss someone's experience of a debilitating illness. That actually says more about the person delivering the platitude than it does about the person with depression.

Stigma, prejudice and discrimination are very much alive and kicking when it comes to this devastating mental health issue.

When I was writing this chapter it reminded me of a story I once heard the comedienne Ruby Wax talk about. Ruby suffered depression for most of her life. She recounted a story whereby her depression got so bad she had to be admitted to a clinic for treatment. She said the whole time she was there she never received one *get well soon* card or a single phone call from the hundreds of people she knew, even though they all knew she was there. She would have received infinitely more sympathy if she had been admitted with two broken legs. Apparently, for some people, depression doesn't really count as a real illness.

If you are reading this and have been experiencing feelings of sadness for an extended period of time it might be an idea to consult with a medical professional so you can be assessed for the early stages of depression. Early assessment can lead to fast and effective treatment while ignoring your symptoms can result in depression that can become deeper and infinitely harder to treat. What have you got to lose by finding out?

What does depression feel like?

Unfortunately, depression is one of those experiences that's nearly impossible to convey accurately through the medium of language. Depression is such a uniquely individual experience it's like trying to describe the color blue to someone that has been blind since birth. No two people suffer this illness in exactly the same way. I will try and convey what it was like based on my own experience of depression; I fully expect your story to be completely different from mine.

Imagine you are standing at the foot of a huge concrete dam. Instead of water, the dam is holding back your emotions. Suddenly, you notice a small hole appearing and now water is starting to trickle out. No big deal you think to yourself and place your hand over the hole. A sense of relief sweeps over you as it appears you have averted a disaster, until you notice another hole appearing. You manage to stem the flow of this one as well, and then another hole appears.

Now you are getting desperate as you are here all alone dealing with the devastation you know is coming. You are shouting for help, but no one is listening. Just when you thought it couldn't get any worse a huge crack opens up in the dam wall. You are feeling weak from the struggle but know you have no choice other than to keep going despite desperately wanting to give up. Then the inevitable happens.

Your dam bursts and you are swept violently downstream by a tsunami of water. You are getting battered off every rock. It's nearly impossible to get your head above water, you feel like you are drowning but somehow you manage to make it to the shore exhausted. You lie there hoping you will never have to go through this again, until it dawns on you that it will be down to you to rebuild the dam brick by brick all by yourself.

This is when the feelings of helplessness, hopelessness, powerlessness and desperation hit—when you realize the enormity of the task ahead of you. Anger, resentment and maybe even self-loathing make an appearance as you start focusing on why life is so bad to you and what did you do to deserve this; after all, you are a good person and you have always been told good things happen to good people.

If you are exceptionally lucky you will be able to rebuild your dam all by yourself, but you will always be plagued by the nagging feeling of *what if* it happens again, how will you cope the next time when you barely survived this time? For some people, their experience will be completely different. They have rebuilt their dams so many times they have now given up completely, unable to fight anymore as they have nothing left to give. They are numb from the struggle and unable to talk about it. They feel so defeated they want to lock themselves away from the world. Is it any wonder they find it difficult to even take a shower they are so weak? If you have never suffered depression, I hope my little story gives you an insight into what life can be like for a sufferer. As you can see the experience is considerably worse than just feeling down in the dumps or sad. Depression can't be snapped out of, wished away or diminished by positive thinking.

Is depression a mental weakness?

It always makes me sad when I hear this question because it normally comes from one of two places, both equally toxic. Sometimes a person can get so low that they start blaming themselves for what is happening in their lives regarding depression. They compare themselves to others and think "everyone else seems happy except me: therefore there must be something wrong with me." This harsh judgment of self can range from "I must have been born with some sort of genetic weakness" to "I must have been evil in a past life, now I am being punished."

I have heard both these statements and a thousand variations in between. They all have one thing in common; they are all wrong. But, to a depressed person, it can feel like there is some veracity to thinking this way. A depressed brain amplifies the inbuilt hardwired bias toward negativity we all have and turns it against us so we start to believe what our mind is telling us without stopping to question if it might actually be false. It can feel like a universal truth that applies to everyone.

Another way someone can believe that their depression is a mental weakness and somehow their fault is when they are told by people on a daily basis to "just snap out of it" or "just think positive" and my personal favorite, "I was depressed myself for a few weeks and just listened to music; now everything is great." There is one thing all these platitudes have in common and that is they trivialize the very real suffering experienced by a depressed person. It tends to make them feel worse, not better. Let's examine these platitudes and decide if they help in any appreciable way.

Just think positive. This is probably the worst piece of advice you can give to a depressed person as it trivializes and dismisses a person's very real suffering in one go. It also displays a profound ignorance on the part of the speaker as depression is not just an absence of positive thinking; it is a thousand times more complex and complicated than that. The depressed person would give their right arm to be able to think positive thoughts; they have lost the ability to do so.

Just snap out of it. I often wonder if the people that utter this statement realize the damage they are doing. I wonder if they actually believe that *just snapping out of it* is actually possible. A depressed person processes this damaging platitude as "I can't snap out of it, therefore, I must be weak." Hardly a recipe for helping someone through the deepest darkest period of their lives, is it?

I was depressed myself once and just listened to music and it all went away. This is just an outright dismissal of the depressed person's experience. They are comparing a case of severe blues to a devastating chronic illness. They are most definitely not comparing like with like. Unfortunately, the depressed mind processes this as "everybody else seems to overcome this easily, there must be something wrong with me." Stop believing the lies you are telling yourself and the lies others are telling you in the form of platitude. Depression is not a mental weakness; you are not to blame for something you have no control over. Don't do that to yourself.

What things do most depressed people have in common?

There will be exceptions to every rule. We are unique and suffer depression in our own unique way. There are however quite a few similarities within that experience that we all share, and here are just a few:

- We all thought depression only happened to *other* people.

- We all thought if it did happen, we could easily overcome it because we were 'mentally strong.'

- We probably ignored all the early stages of depression putting it down to just being tired and maybe irritable from working too hard or not getting enough sleep.

- We might even have dismissed depression in someone else, even telling them to just snap out of it, think positive, pray more or go and get some exercise.

- We have *all* worn a socially acceptable mask to hide our depression.

- We are always great, fine, awesome and on top of the world which also makes us accomplished liars. We are masters of avoiding the issue.

- We have *all* suffered stigma, social isolation, discrimination and prejudice in varying degrees because of our illness.

- We would love to explain to you in detail how we feel, it's not because we don't want to, we don't know how. It's like trying to explain what the color blue is like to a blind person.

- We can feel sometimes that death is preferable to life. Yes, it really is that bad.

- We can feel that we have become observers of our own life, powerless to change and scared of what we have become.

- We want to feel motivated, happy, confident . . . normal. We have lost the ability and lost our way.

- We don't want to be angry, annoyed, self-loathing, reclusive, unhappy and fear the future. Something came along and stole who we were.

What is something that seems helpful to say but actually makes a depressed person feel worse? (Part 1)

I know exactly how you feel. Actually, you don't. There isn't a person on the planet that knows exactly how you feel because pain and suffering are unique to the individual. Even someone that has suffered depression themselves doesn't know how another person feels. At best all they can do is remember how it felt for them and assume it must be the same for you . . . it isn't.

What doesn't kill you makes you stronger. This is platitude at its finest. It's a direct quote from German philosopher Friedrich Nietzsche. While I am quite sure this applies to some other areas in life, depression is not one of those areas. Depression can make someone weaker, not stronger. Saying this to someone suffering depression, shows you don't understand the effect the illness can have on a person.

This too shall pass. How do they know? Can they see into your future? If they can maybe you could ask them exactly *when* it will pass. There is no way of knowing with any certainty how long a period of depression will last and that's what makes it so scary. I personally suffered ten years of depression, but I know innumerable people that have suffered this torment for 20, 30+ years.

Is it really that bad, you look fine to me? Someone suffering depression, is a world-class expert at looking fine when in reality they are dying inside. They have mastered the art of wearing a socially acceptable mask and a pretend smile to disguise the fact they are suffering. Just because someone can't see it doesn't mean it isn't there.

You don't sound depressed. How is a depressed person actually supposed to sound? Are they supposed to sound like Jacob Marley in a Christmas Carol? The person that makes this statement has a stereotypical view of how a depressed person is supposed to sound and behave that bears no resemblance to reality. This answer could be read in conjunction with the previous answer.

You looked fine last week. I think most people imagine that depression is like a straight line. If you were good last week, why aren't you good this week is the implication behind this question? Depression can sometimes come in waves and last week you happened to be on the crest instead of in the hollow. Maybe next week you will be on the way up to the crest again, who knows?

It could be worse, just think about (fill in the blank). This statement has never made any sense to me. How do I comparing myself to people less fortunate than myself help either them or me? If anything it has the potential to make a depressed person feel worse because you have in essence told them they are being selfish and ungrateful for what they have. And while we are on the subject, what are *they* doing to help these poor unfortunate others they want you to feel guilty about?

What is something that seems helpful to say but actually makes a depressed person feel worse? (Part 2)

You're just being selfish. This little gem is normally inflicted on depressed people by members of their direct family. They somehow have the notion that if they can make you feel guilty enough that your depression will magically vanish. It's an attempt at trying to control behavior through negative motivation that has no chance of working. They just don't know it yet.

Just pray more. I have been personally told by a psychiatrist that "if I believed more in the lord I wouldn't be depressed" which begs the question how do they know what I believe in? Also, let's just say I was a staunch believer, this person has now told me that God is punishing me for not having a strong enough faith. Hardly a recipe for a good treatment plan, is it?

Just exercise more. There can be no doubt that exercise can in some cases help with the management of depression. The release of feel-good chemicals into the brain is well documented. However, it has not and will never be a cure for depression. Physical exercise has no impact on how someone views the world. Also, how do you motivate yourself to exercise when all you want to do is sleep because you are so exhausted?

It's just a phase. Normally said to younger people and in some cases maybe it is . . . but do you as a parent want to take the risk of ignoring your child's mental health and have them become a statistic? Teenage suicide rates are on the increase. Don't let your reticence of admitting there might be a problem become a block to getting help. Don't gamble with someone else's well-being.

What have you got to be depressed about? Normally said in a condescending or judgmental tone. This normally comes from someone that thinks all depression is created equally and there has to be a *reason* for being depressed. There doesn't have to be an event or trigger for depression to come into someone's life. That's why when someone suffering depression is asked this question the normal response is, "I don't know why?" because they don't.

I don't believe in depression. Who cares what you believe in? Depression exists and is a reality for millions upon millions of people worldwide. Hopefully, if you are extremely lucky you won't get to experience it up close and personal. Actually, this reminds me of those people that thought COVID-19 didn't exist. I don't think I need to say anymore.

Aren't you ashamed? Ashamed of what, being unfortunate enough to have an illness that you never invited into your life and have tremendous difficulty coping with? If you are hearing this from someone, they are a person who is obsessed with what others think of them. I can think of at least two countries where this would be the common response to the revelation you have depression. Hopefully, you are not in one of those countries.

What is something that seems helpful to say but actually makes a depressed person feel worse? (Part 3)

Just think positive. Have you ever been given bad news and tried not to acknowledge its existence by ignoring it? What happens? That's correct; it forces its way into your psyche until you have no other option than to take notice. That's what depression does; it forces itself into the mind and no amount of positive thinking will counteract it. Doing so is the equivalent of pretending it doesn't exist in the hope it goes away. It *never* works long term. Positive thinking is a game of kinesthetic denial. In other words, you try and make yourself feel better by positive thinking, but don't actually address the underlying issue.

Just forget about it. Let's try a little experiment, try not to think of a black horse. Come on! How difficult can it be? Just forget about a black horse. Telling someone to forget their depression is like telling someone with a broken leg to forget about the pain. It actually focuses the mind on the problem and makes it worse, not better.

Just snap out of it. I decided to save the best for last. To those that are tempted to say this to someone suffering depression, I plead with you to tell us all exactly *how* to *snap out of it*. I have yet to meet someone that just *snapped* out of long-term serious depression. I sincerely wish I knew how to get people to snap out of depression as I would become a multibillionaire overnight. If you have snapped out of long-term depression, I apologize to you and humbly ask you to share your secret—with details.

I could probably go on for another few hours with these. Ok, maybe a few more then. You need to eat more vegetables, take medication, stop your medication, why do you hate yourself so much? Why have you not tried feeling better? Why are you wasting your life? It's all in your head, drink plenty of fluids, get a hobby, socialize more, I was depressed myself once for a week, stop feeling sorry for yourself, and another personal favorite, don't tell anyone; they will think you are mad.

If you are suffering depression you are going to be sick to the teeth of hearing all of the above and will have to grow a thicker skin. I think most people don't know what to say when confronted with depression, so a platitude fills the gap nicely.

All of the above have one thing in common; they diminish, minimize and make light of the very real suffering the other person is going through. Whether this is done knowingly or unknowingly is anyone's guess. I am quite sure some people think it's funny to trivialize another's suffering. Frankly, that says a lot more about them than it does about you. A piece of advice, if you encounter *any* of the above, please don't fall into the trap of trying to justify yourself as you are going to come off as looking for validation. Just don't go there. Smile, nod your head and walk away. Your job is about trying to get better, not trying to defend yourself.

Which signs of depression can go unnoticed?

Actually, most of the signs of depression can go unnoticed for quite a while.

I have on countless occasions asked people when they first noticed they were depressed. Most people will say within the last six to nine months, but on closer investigation, it is obvious their depression started years before. They only noticed it once their symptoms became *considerably* worse and it was affecting their lives. It had crept up on them insidiously.

They put the tiredness, apathy, loss of interest, etc. down to working too much or maybe not sleeping properly—it can take a while before someone joins the dots. It's quite common for someone else to point out they may be suffering from depression before they see it in themselves and take action.

I can't stress forcefully enough how important it is to get treatment for depression at the earliest possible stage as time has the habit of making this illness harder to treat as it allows it to become deeper and more pervasive. What have you got to lose by making an appointment with your doctor and discussing how you are feeling? If you are reading this book, it is *definitely* time to make an appointment.

A *wait and see* approach is not something you want to do when it comes to your mental health. I completely understand that it is difficult to put your hand up and admit you might be having problems. Society has taught us well that we should just keep our problems to ourselves and suck it up—especially men.

Apathy and lack of motivation are two of the biggest symptoms of depression. Unfortunately, you have to overcome these very difficult symptoms to get the help you need. There is no other way. You have absolutely got to be proactive. If you can't bring yourself to make that phone call, get someone else to do it for you. Find a way.

Never ignore wanting to hurt yourself. If you are feeling like the world would be a better place without you it's time to pay attention. Self-harm is always a sign of something deeper. You need to talk to someone as soon as possible.

If you bounce between feeling good and then feeling terrible for days or maybe even weeks on end it is time to get proactive and take some action. These waves of depression rarely go away on their own and could be a sign of a more serious type of depression like bipolar.

Fantasizing or even planning to end your own life? I don't think there is a human on the planet that hasn't thought the words "I wish I was dead" at least once in their lives. It's when those idle thoughts become constant and move on to suicidal ideation that you really need to become concerned. Ideation should be treated as an emergency.

Physical pain and depression walk hand in hand. If you have been injured or you are suffering some kind of long-term painful illness you need to pay close attention to your mood as depression can easily slip in unnoticed because of your focus on the pain.

What are some differences between depressed and non-depressed people?

I won't go into all the medical symptoms surrounding depression as they are very well known. Instead, here are some of the things not so commonly talked about that make living with depression intolerable:

- A normal person doesn't have to pretend to be normal; a depressed person has to pretend and wear a socially acceptable mask every day.

- A normal person feels like they have a life; a depressed person can feel like theirs is on hold.

- A normal person doesn't have to cope with never-ending feelings of hopelessness, worthlessness and helplessness; a depressed person can feel like that every day.

- A normal person can have dreams about the future; a depressed person's dreams are lying in tatters in the gutter.

- A depressed person feels trapped by their own mind, unable to shake free from their illness.

- A normal person doesn't have to explain their illness a thousand times, and still be misunderstood.

- A normal person can feel like their life has meaning and purpose; a depressed person can feel like their life has neither.

- A normal person participates in life; a depressed person can feel like an observer constantly stuck on the outside looking in.

- A normal person can feel like there is a reason to get out of bed in the morning; a depressed person can struggle to find *any* reason.

- A normal person doesn't commit suicide because they feel normal; depressed people can and do commit suicide because they are depressed.

- A normal person can feel like their life is just beginning; a depressed person can feel like their life is already over.

- A normal person can feel happy; a depressed person contrary to popular belief wants to be happy, they just don't know how.

- A normal person doesn't have to contend with prejudice and stigma because they are feeling ill; a depressed person does. Daily.

- A normal person isn't made to feel like they are *faking* it if they are ill; a depressed person can feel this constantly.

- A normal person can enjoy the company of others; for a depressed person that same company can be a nightmare.

- A normal person can view life through rose-tinted glasses; a depressed person's glasses only come in one shade, crap-colored.

Please don't get upset over the word *normal*; I am not insinuating that depressed people are not normal. It just looked better than the word *depressed* and *non-depressed* getting repeated twice in the same sentence.

What are some habits that make depression worse?

This answer will seem like somewhat of a contradiction.

The things that can make depression *feel* worse are the very things a depressed person finds next to impossible *not to do*—such is the nature of the illness.

- Oversleeping is not a great way to feel better but is a great way to escape the non-relenting torment that a depressed person has to go through, even if it is only for a few hours.

- Isolation. Staying away from other people has an obvious detrimental effect, but it also means you don't have to explain your illness and be misunderstood for the billionth time. It also means you can throw your socially acceptable mask into the bin for a few hours.

- Canceling activities at the last minute. Let's face it being social and putting on a brave face is the *last* thing a depressed person wants to do; it simply requires too much effort. The mask has to come out of the bin again and the pretense has to begin.

- Self-medicating with alcohol or drugs. Depressed or not, everybody knows this is not a good idea and can lead to even bigger problems than depression. However, a person in the depths of despair will do *anything* to escape the suffering. Future consequences are very low on the list at this time.

- Overeating. I don't know about you but when I was depressed, I would have eaten the wallpaper. There is no disputing the fact that eating high-calorie food makes you feel better temporarily, and that's what we are after—no matter how short the duration. Dieting is for another time.

Telling people you are fine when you are not. What are you supposed to do? If you tell people you are depressed like society tells us to do, you run the very real possibility of social exclusion, prejudice, stigma and discrimination.

Just so we are clear, I am not advocating any of the above as a way to cope with depression. I am merely pointing out that with depression it is rarely as clear-cut as don't do this, don't do that.

If you read the list again carefully, you will notice that no concern for the future or adverse consequences is a very common thread. Depressed people suffer in the here and now. When they think of the future they just imagine more of the same, so can you really blame them for wanting to take away a little bit of the pain, no matter how briefly?

You can subsequently see that all of the above tend to make depression feel worse, but it can temporarily make someone feel better no matter how much of a contradiction it appears to be to a non-depressed observer.

What are some things you wish others knew about depression?

I could probably keep you reading for the next hour answering this question, but I will restrict myself to some of the most significant ones.

All depression is not created equal. Generally, I think when most people hear the word depression, they incorrectly assume that it is all the same and that everybody suffers it in the exact same manner. Nothing could be further from the truth. I can guarantee there won't be a person on the planet that has/is suffering depression that hasn't heard a version of "Oh, I was depressed myself once and I just snapped myself out of it." I don't think so! Severe depression can't be snapped out of, prayed away, exercised away or eradicated by sheer force of will. It simply doesn't function that way.

Serious depression requires serious intervention by serious professionals. If someone tells you they *just snapped out of it* the person you are talking to has obviously never experienced the horrors of severe depression, bipolar depression or major depressive disorder. If they had, they would never make such a statement.

Depression is self-inflicted. Depression happens *to* a person. They didn't wake up one morning and decide it might be a good idea to inflict a potentially life-changing illness on themselves. There isn't a depressed person anywhere that doesn't wish things were different and they didn't have to battle with this unseen monster on a daily basis. They are not in this predicament by sheer choice; it has been forced upon them. Depressed people want to be happy; they have lost the ability to be so.

It's not easy asking for help. Asking for help is probably the hardest thing a depressed person finds doing. That's why it takes so long for them to eventually turn up at a mental health professional's door. It's not easy putting your hand up and admitting you may have a mental health issue. I have nothing but the deepest respect for those people that have taken self-responsibility and admitted that *for now*, they are unable to cope and need some professional intervention.

Making fun of someone suffering depression. Making fun of someone suffering depression by calling them a fake or just looking for attention says a lot more about the person doing the talking than it does about the person doing the suffering. It takes a particularly small-minded person to laugh at someone that is experiencing real pain and suffering on a scale most people can only imagine.

Popping pills is the answer. Contrary to popular belief depression sufferers don't just pop a pill and suddenly everything becomes better. It isn't a headache they have. They won't be walking around tomorrow smiling because they have taken some medication. It takes time and patience to overcome this illness. Granted, some people recover faster than others but that has nothing to do with willpower or determination. For some people, medication can be a life-saver, for others, not so much.

Depression only affects some types of people. Depression is equal opportunities. It doesn't care about the color of your skin, how much money you have, how religious you are or how intelligent you are—it can happen at any time and any age to anyone. There is no way to guard against it happening. If it decides to come knocking on your door (life), it's something a person has to accept and deal with. Denying it is happening is probably the worst thing someone can do as the illness insidiously invades a person's life getting worse in the background and making it harder to treat. In the case of depression, reaching out sooner rather than later has the potential to pay huge dividends.

What do depressed people suffer that other people take for granted? (Part 1)

Crippling indecision. Depressed people can be consumed by an overwhelming inability to make decisions. Everything is questioned right down to the granular level. This constant self-questioning and evaluating leaves the person paralyzed and unable to function. For instance, the depressed person might decide to take a shower. What follows next is a tsunami of questions: "Should I wait until later?" "What if I don't have the energy?" "Why do I need a shower anyhow; I am not going anywhere?" This can literally play out for hours and hours until the sufferer finally says something along the lines of "What's the point?" Needless to say this self-doubting will be followed by recrimination and more than likely self-hatred for being so weak, which in turn feeds the depression, an almost perfect vicious circle.

Critical self-judgment. Depressed people don't really see themselves as ill. They rarely give themselves that good a break. Instead, they can very easily view their depression as a personal weakness they could overcome if they just tried hard enough. This train of thought is perpetuated by other people telling them to *just snap out of it,* or a thousand other platitudes they have heard a million times before. Instead of seeing this nonsense for what it really is, they turn it internally and berate themselves for having a character flaw that doesn't allow them to function like *normal* people. They don't need other people to be judgmental as they are experts at doing it to themselves a thousand times worse.

Interaction is painful. It's something most people take for granted. Interaction, conversing and relating are things we mostly don't have to think about. For someone suffering depression, this natural ability can become excruciatingly difficult. In most instances, we pull on a socially acceptable mask and pretend everything is fine. We are present but not really there if you know what I mean? We can be surrounded by people and feel painfully alone—lost in the quicksand of depression. We are experts at hearing but not really listening. We are ninja warriors at the art of avoiding talking about how we are feeling. Everything is great and fine when in reality we are dying inside. While you are talking about how your day went, we can be reliving the worst moments of ours and at the same time making sure you don't see our pain.

Fear of the future. Ask a depressed person what they think their future looks like and they will more than likely tell you, "More of the same or worse." Depending on the severity of the depression a sufferer doesn't see a future. A future is something other people have not them. Their future is the struggle they are going to have tomorrow morning when they wake up and think to themselves, "Please, not this again, I don't think I can go on like this." We think about the future by comparing it to our past. It's very difficult to imagine a nice future when all the evidence from the past is telling you it isn't going to happen. For the vast majority of people, a future is something they can feel optimistic about. For a depressed person, it can feel like something to dread. Something filled with hopelessness and helplessness. Not living in the present is extremely common; it can feel like we are adrift in an ocean of misery and torment—stuck in a no man's land of despair and apathy. Once hope is lost, everything is lost.

What do depressed people suffer that other people take for granted? (Part 2)

Even the good times can be bad. Imagine not even being happy at the birth of your child or in fact any landmark occasion that marks a supposedly joyous event in our lives. A chronically depressed person doesn't have to imagine it. For millions of people, this is a reality and is something incredibly difficult to come to terms with. Guilt and shame which feed the depression are experienced in equal measure. They know on a rational logical level they *should* be happy, but unfortunately, they have lost the ability. Their happiness has been replaced by numbness and indifference which they have seemingly no control over. I well remember when I was going through my own depression someone asking me what I would do if I won a million pounds. Without even having to think, I said I would probably give it away as no amount of money could ever make me happy again. These are the depths a depressed mind can sink to.

Observing not participating. There is a song from the movie *Midnight Cowboy* sung by Harry Nilsson that I think sums up depression beautifully. Here it is. "Everybody's talking at me, I don't hear a word they're saying only the echoes of my mind." Severe depression is probably like having an out-of-body experience. You can see and hear everything happening around you, but you are not part of it. It can feel very lonely and isolating to realize that you are a spectator to your own life. Your heart aches to be part of something that will make you feel like a human being again, but your depressed mind is constantly telling you that this is for other people to experience, not you. Just like the song, you literally do hear what everybody is saying but you are lost in a mire of the echoes of your own mind. It can feel like you are living a life where the pause button is permanently pressed. A state of non-existing if you like.

Dysfunctional relating and relationships. It's no coincidence that the rate of breakups and divorces amongst people suffering depression is quite high. Relating to another human being requires motivation that is sadly lacking as they struggle with their illness. Maintaining relationships requires effort and energy both of which have been sucked out of them. It's not that they don't care; it's because they have lost the ability to care, and they feel powerless to do anything about it. When you don't care if you live or die yourself it can be very difficult to care for someone else. They are trapped inside the prison of their own mind—desperately hoping for someone or something to set them free. For a depressed person isolating themselves can be preferable to relating even though they absolutely know this is doing them real harm. A depressed mind doesn't think rationally; it will push away the very thing that could help them. It can see relationships as having very little consequence, even though the opposite is true—such is the contradictory nature of depression.

Lack of autonomy. The most important thing to every human being on the planet is having a sense of autonomy or control over their lives. When depression comes into a person's life that sense of control is taken away. Choices start to become very limited, and the person's world can become microscopic. In an effort to fill that emotional void many people turn to food, alcohol, drugs, shopping anything—in fact, anything that alleviates, however temporarily, the crushing feeling of being out of control of their own destiny. These strategies can of course bring about bigger problems to add to the depression. A sense of meaning or purpose to their lives is missing and in its place is a gaping hole. This can set some people off on a journey to find that missing piece in the vain hope that it will complete them. They never find that *thing* that will make them whole again because it doesn't exist. It is a depression-generated wild goose chase that can easily turn into an obsession. Depression holds out the promise that if you could just find that thing outside yourself everything would return to normal, and the depression would vanish. Unfortunately, as many people have found to their cost, including myself, it's simply not true. The answer lies internally not externally.

There are countless different ways that people can experience depression. There are however quite a few commonalities between the different types. If any of the above resonated with you it's time to seek professional help. These types of symptoms won't be exercised away, prayed away, snapped out of or ignored. If left unaddressed, they have the ability to devastate your life for a very long period of time.

What is the internal monologue of a depressed person?

To put it politely it's not good. I want to apologize in advance for the swear words I use in this chapter; it is merely done to make a point. If someone said out loud what they actually say to themselves, they would probably get arrested. The inner language of a depressed person is generally denigrating, berating, judgmental and critical. It can also vary depending on the day they are having. So if you don't like swear words you might want to skip this chapter. Here we go.

On a reasonably good day.

- Maybe I will try a bit of exercise that everybody keeps telling me to do. I'm still feeling a bit tired though. Maybe I will give it a go tomorrow when I'm feeling better. Yes, that's it. I will definitely do it tomorrow . . . or maybe the day after.

- Not feeling bad today, maybe I'm not depressed anymore. If I feel like this tomorrow, I might stop taking those anti-depressants. I hope it doesn't return; maybe this time will be different.

- Look at the state of this place! I need to get it into some sort of order. I will do it after I have a bit of sleep. Maybe someone else will do it for me? I will wait and see if I am better tomorrow and do it then . . . maybe.

A bad day.

- I knew it wouldn't f*king last. I feel f*king terrible. What a weak loser; nothing ever goes right for me. I'm going to be like this for the rest of my f*king life. What did I ever do to deserve this? I might as well go back to my bed—I won't be missed anyhow. Nobody gives a crap whether I am alive or dead.

- F*k that therapy! It's a waste of time and they can shove their medication as well. All it does is make me feel worse. It seems to work for everybody else. You worthless piece of s**t! Why not me? I would be better off dead. That way I won't be a burden to everybody. My whole body hurts. Please, please shut the f*k up!

- Why does everybody hate me? I need to shower but what's the f*king point? It won't make me feel any better and I am exhausted. I wish I could go to sleep and never wake up again . . . I wonder would anyone miss me? I wish I could turn off that f*king voice.

A really bad day.

- I wish everybody would leave me the f*k alone; nobody understands how I feel. I wonder does it hurt to die? I wonder would anyone care if I killed myself? You won't kill yourself; you're too much of a coward.

- If only I could change what happened, why me? What's life about anyhow? It's just one miserable f*king day after another with no end. How do people live like this? I certainly can't/won't?

- Nothing's going to change the way I feel. I'm not sure I want to get better anyhow. Maybe I deserve to be punished? That f*king voice is killing me. What's the big deal with suicide anyhow, who would give a f*k? I'm going to do it.

Shocking, isn't it? This is a daily reality for millions of people around the world, and I was one of those people. I said all of this and a whole lot worse. I realized I needed help when I was sitting at a railway crossing with my foot hovering over the accelerator of the car wondering if my passenger would survive the impact of the collision. It was probably the only thing that stopped me.

My advice has always been the same the whole way through this book. Get help and get it now! This intensity of depression never goes away on its own. Forget anything you have heard/read/or been told about saying that exercise or positive thinking will eliminate this torture—it won't. Make an appointment and make it today! Good luck.

I am tired of being depressed and I am ready to end it, what should I do?

First, understand that you are not alone and hundreds of thousands if not millions of people have been here before, myself included.

Depression can absolutely make someone feel like there are no options, no choices no way out, no hope. It's the nature of this distressing illness.

But there are options, there is hope; but then again you have to want to go out and find it with every fiber of your body. You need to talk to someone about how you are feeling because you don't really have the capacity to talk yourself out of your current situation. The reason you can't is because you will be trying to use the same mind that got you into depression in the first place, and it wants you to stay stuck in this rut.

This mind isn't going to help you as it has become familiar with the status quo and wants to keep things the same because it loves patterns and consistency—not change.

It requires professional help to lead you out of this maze which I sincerely hope you go and find. I have no idea which country you are in but a visit to your doctor would probably be a good starting point and then take it from there.

You are a seriously awesome human being (even though you feel the complete opposite) for sharing what you did that required courage. Now use some of that courage that you just proved you have and take the next proactive step by making an appointment.

If things have gotten that bad that you can't wait to be seen by your doctor, can I suggest you go to the back of this book and call the suicide hotline in the country you reside in. If that's not an option, please go to your nearest hospital. Go straight to their accident and emergency department (because this is an emergency) and tell them what you are contemplating. They are obligated to help you.

You need to reach out and you need to do it now. Please don't wait until tomorrow to see if things get better. Don't gamble with your life and mental health, you are worth more than that.

If you are so depressed why not just choose happiness?

If you have ever been asked this question one thing is for certain, the person asking the question is demonstrating a profound ignorance as to how depression actually affects someone. They are also implying that you are choosing depression over happiness. Let's get real. Who in their right mind would choose something as debilitating as depression over happiness? If it were as simple as making a choice, 350 million people would be cured overnight.

The fact is a depressed person would like nothing more than to be happy again. They don't enjoy feelings of hopelessness, helplessness, worthlessness and despair. They are not choosing to be depressed—depression has been inflicted upon them and their choice to be happy again has been taken away. They had absolutely no say in the matter. People endure depression in the hope that things will get better. They are not rejecting happiness—their illness is ensuring that happiness isn't even an option. I think an analogy might help get some perspective on this question.

Imagine you are a keen mountain climber, and your ambition is to climb Mount Everest. You have trained for years, and the day finally arrives as you set off from base camp determined to conquer the summit. Everything is going well until you hear a rumbling far above you. It's the thing all climbers fear the most; an avalanche. You see this tsunami of snow headed in your direction, but you are powerless to do anything about it. No matter which way you run, it's going to hit hard. It hits and you are buried under 100 feet of snow with this immense pressure and weight bearing down on you. You start to struggle only to find you are stuck—unable to move so much as a finger. It isn't long before a sense of helplessness starts to creep in. The weight keeps bearing down and the harder you try to get out the weaker you become until eventually, tired from the struggle, you just give up.

That's the reality of depression for an awful lot of people.

They can't just dig themselves out. They are stuck, unable to move or help themselves. If they are extremely lucky someone might come along and help move some of the weight off of them so they can mobilize again. Until that time, they can feel like they are going to be like this forever and can easily descend into something called learned helplessness. They want to dig themselves out, but they have lost the ability. Finding happiness for them is like trying to find a shovel in our proverbial avalanche—you know it's there you just can't find it.

Depression is never a straightforward binary choice between being happy or unhappy nor is the person to blame for their predicament which the question not so subtly implies. It would be the equivalent of blaming our climber for getting buried in all that snow. Depression is a formidable opponent that first makes sure you are unable to fight by taking away all your motivation and energy. One last thing I would leave our questioner to ponder. How exactly do you maintain a constant state of happiness all day every day to keep depression at bay? Depression isn't sadness; it's an illness.

Why depressed people isolate themselves, and why it's not a good idea?

What follows is strictly my experience with isolating during episodes of depression. I fully expect as with everything concerning depression that your experience might be completely different. However, when I have mentioned this to people that have/are suffering depression it's quite amazing how many people have gone through exactly the same thing. I would add that it is probably more common with reactive/situational depression.

We are the creators of our own experiences; in other words, our thoughts and beliefs create emotions that we respond to. We are in effect creating our own depressive experiences. And if you don't believe that to be true then ask yourself who else could be creating these experiences and how do they get into your body? Certainly, someone can create an event that is not of our making but how we respond to that event *is* of our making. Please note that nowhere did I mention we are to blame for how we are feeling.

Anyhow, when I was depressed, I realize now with the benefit of hindsight that when I isolated what I was in actual fact looking for was emotional protection. I reckoned that if I built an emotional wall high enough and deep enough I would be protected from the emotional demon that I called depression. If I kept everyone at arm's length and didn't have to interact with other people that somehow the unseen demon would remain the other side of my emotional barrier. Little did I realize that what I had actually done, because I created my experiences, was trapping the demon behind the wall with me and isolating myself made me feel considerably worse instead of better. I had to fight that unseen dark force on my own, and it normally won leaving me drained and feeling hopeless. Depression can feel like an abusive relationship. It can tell you to isolate yourself for your own good when in reality what it wants is control and to keep you to itself.

Ironically, depression makes us feel that isolation is a good idea when actually trying to be a bit more sociable would work considerably better for us—no matter how counter-intuitive that might seem. We rationalize that isolation is a good idea because we don't want to be a burden on other people but that is the depression talking to us. It tells us we *are* being a burden to others. If only we had enough strength to see through this deception. Isolation keeps us behind that wall creating the same self-hating scenarios over and over again inside our heads—making us weaker while at the same time making our unseen demon stronger.

A little word of warning and this is something I also found out to my own detriment. A depressed mind is inclined to think in black and white with no shades of grey in between. So you could be reading this and thinking, "all I need to do is throw myself lock stock and barrel into something that keeps me busy." No, that is not the answer; it's just another way of distracting yourself from what is really going on. You need to find a balance between the two and be aware if you are crossing the line into either distraction or isolation. Believe me when I say this is a very difficult thing to do. Your mind will be naturally drawn to the familiarity of isolation. It takes enormous strength to do the opposite of what every sinew in your body is telling you especially if this self-abuse has been going on for a while.

Alternative views on isolation

As you have just read my experiences with isolation during depression, I thought I might give some insight into why other people isolate themselves during periods of deep depression.

Not wanting people to know. It can seem easier to lock themselves away from other people than trying to hide the very real suffering someone is experiencing. Sometimes people get tired of having to wear a socially acceptable mask and pretend they are fine when in actual fact they are in a world of torment. Unfortunately, in our attempt to hide the truth from other people it can make other people even more inquisitive as to why we are becoming a recluse. It can become a real catch 22 situation.

Feelings of being a failure or not good enough. This can be a very powerful motivator for people to remove themselves from public view especially if the person concerned was originally an outgoing type of personality or they viewed themselves as having their life together. Never underestimate the power of stigma and other people's judgments when it comes to suffering depression. We haven't evolved yet to the point that we can discuss mental health issues as easily as we talk about something that was on television last night. Should it be that way? No, it shouldn't, but it is.

Introspection. At face value, introspection seems like it might be a good idea. The person retreats into seclusion to battle with the unseen demon. What they fail to realize is they are taking a toothpick to a knife fight. They are trying to use a mind that is caught in a downward spiral of negativity against the very thing that is causing the negativity. It normally makes matters worse instead of better.

Protecting others. If you ask a thousand people that suffer depression why they isolate, the number one answer would probably be: "I don't want to be a burden on other people." They can very easily assume that their negativity will somehow infect the other person. I understand if you are reading this you could well be thinking it doesn't make any sense. That's the thing about depression; it can turn rational thought into very irrational thought in the blink of an eye. It makes perfect sense when you are doing it.

Interaction with others. Make no mistake, people that suffer depression can find it excruciatingly difficult to interact with other people. Trying to put on an act of being sociable can amount to an emotionally painful experience. It gets tiring having to be on their guard all of the time and having to make sure that the socially acceptable mask they are wearing doesn't slip and reveal who they *really* are. It isn't much fun being in a social setting surrounded by happy people when you are feeling like the loneliest person on the planet.

There is a myriad of reasons why someone with depression feels the need to isolate themselves, and I have given you probably five of the most popular reasons. Isolation can be a double-edged sword. On the one hand, it can feel like it helps in the moment, while on the other hand, it can deepen the sense of being misunderstood that sufferers so often feel. The lure of isolation can become very familiar and also a very difficult habit to break.

Is fighting depression a good idea?

Yes. Because no one else is going to fight it for you.

Ultimately, it's going to be down to you.

I know this is something most depressed people don't want to hear; it's not easy to fight when the fight has already been kicked out of you. But, there's still a little flicker of a flame that was once you, still waiting inside to be fanned into life.

That tiny flicker might only start out by making a phone call, reading a page of a book or walking one hundred yards—anything that starts even in the smallest way to break the deathly grip depression has. What is the absolutely smallest thing you could do starting today that could set you on the road to recovery? Set a timer to five minutes and start that thing you have been putting off for so long. Forget about the long haul—start small.

I have always thought of depression as the silent illness. It just sits there in the background eating at your very core from the inside out, until what remains is a husk of the person you once were. Is there hope? There's always hope, but you are the one that has to go out and bring it into your life. Some people might help you along the way.

Therapists, parents, friends and family *can* be a source of help, and sometimes they can even be a pothole on the road to your recovery. Ultimately, you are the one that has to travel this road alone, you are the one that has to start the journey by taking the very first step, you are the one that has to nurture and fan that tiny flame back into life when you would rather hide in a corner and die.

Depression needs to be a proactive illness. Inactivity allows it to fester and spread into unexpected areas of your life. Believe me; I know how hard this is going to be. I suffered ten years of depression myself. What I am asking you to do is the equivalent of running 100 meters with a broken leg. But, keep looking at what potentially awaits you at the finish line—it will be painful, but worth it.

I can nearly hear you saying, *"Yes, but . . ."* That's what depression does; it sucks the life out of you and provides you with plausible reasons to remain in the same place. You will need plenty of resolve to ignore that voice of depression and take the first step. It hurts me to write this stuff, and I would love to be able to sugar-coat this painful truth for you. Unfortunately, this is probably what you have been getting up until now, and it's keeping you stuck.

I was caught in this quagmire for years. I had a serious accident that has resulted in me being in constant pain. The depression had convinced me that there was *no point* in getting treatment or even trying to help myself because I would still have the pain. It took a long time and a lot of convincing to realize that pain and depression were two separate entities and needed to be treated as such. Depression is a liar that convinces you it is telling the truth. What lies is depression telling you that makes it difficult to move past *what's the point* and have you ever truly examined these lies?

What prevents some people from seeking help for depression?

I understand it can seem like a counter-intuitive concept, because after all why wouldn't someone want to reach out for help if they are depressed? There can be several reasons for this. Naturally, I can't give you *all* the reasons but here are some of the most popular ones. Hopefully, some of them will strike a chord with you.

I shouldn't feel this way. This is particularly common amongst those people that see themselves as strong-willed or very independent. For those types, depression is perceived by themselves as a weakness or a character flaw that should be easily overcome by applying themselves to the problem. Unfortunately, they soon find out that depression is not like solving a mechanical problem with a car.

I should be able to cope with this on my own. Unfortunately, what they don't realize is that they are trying to use the same mind that is now caught in a whirlwind of negativity against the mind that caused the depression in the first place. They are in essence fighting themselves from a position of weakness. Self-medicating with drugs, food or alcohol is very common and can lead to even further complications in the future.

I should be grateful for what I have. If this mindset were actually true it would mean that the person suffering depression is only doing so because they are selfish, and the cure would be to adopt an attitude of gratitude. This *might* work for someone that is feeling a little bit down, but it won't work for someone suffering serious depression. Depression is an illness; it is not brought about by being ungrateful or solved by being thankful.

I will wait a while longer. Sadly, this is something that is extremely common. For some people depression can be episodic, in other words, it can come in waves. They might be depressed for a period of time and then it passes. In this remission time, they can become convinced that it is gone for good only for it to return at a later time. This oscillation allows the depression to become deeper and harder to treat in the future.

What have I got to be depressed about? Again, this goes back to the concept of being selfish that I talked about earlier. This person is convinced there must be a *reason* for being depressed; this is not the case at all. If you go back and read the chapter on the different types of depression you will see quite a few of them don't need a reason or triggering event to show up in someone's life.

I should just man/woman up. Exactly how does someone man/woman up? I have never read an article in forty years that sets out how it is actually achieved and how it helps with depression. This is a society-generated concept where a mental health issue is perceived as a weakness or a character flaw that can be vanquished by being tough on ourselves. All it does is show a profound ignorance of how depression actually works.

In the next chapter, we will get into the fears that prevent people from reaching out.

What fears prevent some people from seeking help for depression?

What will other people think of me? I would counter this question with another question. Are you going to let what other people think of you dictate your mental health? The truth is you can't stop someone from thinking whatever they want. Another truth is that people are so concerned with what is going on in their own lives you will barely register unless you are directly impacting them. We are just not that important to other people.

What will my doctor/therapist think? Not a lot actually, because they have heard it all before and probably several times that day. The job of a professional is to evaluate and treat and not to sit in judgment. If you are unfortunate to come across someone that does sit in judgment it should be a clear indication that you need to find yourself someone that doesn't. Don't think twice about changing therapists if you feel they aren't a good fit.

Someone told me therapy doesn't work. No, what someone told you is that therapy didn't work for *them*; it does not follow that it won't work for you. Therapy is a very nuanced process that requires a lot of input from the patient. Certainly, therapy won't help for all people but that doesn't mean that therapy is ineffective. In the vast majority of cases, it is very effective. Make an informed decision and find out for yourself.

Maybe I am just faking it. Highly unlikely as serious depression is extremely difficult to fake. What is more likely is that you have adapted to your depression, and it might not be as bad as it was in the beginning. That doesn't mean it has gone away; it just means you are tolerating it better. People worrying they are faking depression is an extremely common experience. Would you not be better off getting a professional opinion?

I wouldn't know what to say. You don't need to know what to say; this is not a job interview. The professional sitting opposite you is well aware this is all new to you and will do everything they can to put you at ease. Their job is to guide you and not interrogate you. Just show up and be yourself. Initially, that is all that is required of you. Someone is paying this professional to do the heavy lifting, let them do what they are getting paid for.

Have you noticed a common theme running through all of the above? They are stories we are telling ourselves that are keeping us stuck. We never stop and actually question whether these self-generated stories are actually true. We have repeated them so many times to ourselves that we have come to accept them as truth. Fear of the unknown can be a powerful demotivator and we alleviate this fear by justifying our decisions with logic. Are you doing this? Are you telling yourself that maybe your issues are not that important, or you are just being silly? Maybe it's time to question that assertion.

One last thing that can hold people back from seeking help is the thought that they don't want to talk about *all* their perceived secrets. The reality is a skilled therapist won't push you any further than you are comfortable with. There is no requirement to tell them everything in the first session. You dictate the speed at which things happen.

Why do some people treat depression like it's something you can easily get over or just think that you're being moody?

I would like you to think back to the people that thought depression was easy to get over and that you were just being moody. What do they all have in common? What they all have in common is that not one of them has ever suffered depression. How do I know that having never met any of them? The answer is very simple. Nobody that has ever suffered the torture that is depression would ever consider making such a statement.

If you are ever unfortunate to come across one of these people again, I would ask them the following question: "How do you know that depression is easy to get over it if you have never suffered it yourself?" At this point, you will either be met with stunned silence or a retort that goes something along the lines of "Oh, I was depressed myself one time for a few weeks and just snapped out of it." You have your fish on the line, now it's time to reel them in. At this point, you just say, "Really, which of the ten diagnosable types of depression did you suffer?" Game, set, and match, go and collect your trophy!

The truth is what you are experiencing here is a clash of semantics. To you, the word depression means a serious mental health issue that you are struggling with. To the other person, the word depression is nothing more than feeling a bit down. They are under the illusion that the two are exactly the same, which of course they aren't. Unfortunately, the word depression has become meaningless; it can mean anything from being suicidal to something as trivial as being *depressed* because someone didn't send them a text in time. Is it any wonder there is so much confusion?

Okay, so now you know why the person said what they said and a potential tongue-in-cheek answer to give them we are ready to move on to the most important part. And that is what are you going to do about it the next time? The way I see it you have two options. You can either educate this person all about depression or you can shrug your shoulders and move on. Believe it or not, I think the latter is the solution you need to go for and here is why.

If you decided you are going to educate this person, I would ask you to ponder these questions first. What do you hope to achieve? What's in this for you? Why do you feel the need to educate this person? Do you honestly think this person is going to allow you to change a belief they have about depression and admit that maybe they were wrong? This is never going to happen. People are very difficult to shift from long-held beliefs and will defend them vigorously even if they know they are wrong. Do you really want the aggravation of trying to educate someone that is not listening? Be very careful if you decide to go this route that you don't end up trying to convince the other person that when it comes to depression you are the real deal. You are going to feel worse, not better, and they still won't change their belief. So that leaves you with option two.

Shrugging your shoulders and walking away is something your ego doesn't want you to do. It wants you to put this person in their place. You have to ignore this nagging voice and do what's best for you, and that isn't trying to teach the unteachable.

Is there a way to make depression symptoms better without getting help?

I want you to think long and hard about this for a moment. The most common symptoms of depression, which are very well known and covered in detail in the book, are only an external manifestation of something happening a lot deeper. Think of depression being a bit like an iceberg. The bit that is visible is only a very small part of the whole picture. If someone decides to use positive thinking for instance to cope with the symptoms, they have fallen headfirst into the trap of kinesthetic denial. What is kinesthetic denial?

Kinesthetic denial is where someone uses a technique to make themselves feel temporarily better in the moment but doesn't address the underlying issue that is at the root cause of their problems. A very simple example of this would be someone using alcohol to help with their chronic social anxiety. The alcohol might allow them to function at a certain level, but it will never address whatever it is that is driving their anxiety.

A good comparison with depression is when someone uses sleeping tablets to help with the insomnia that is so common with depression. The tablets will certainly give them a *form* of sleep but unless the underlying problems are addressed getting a proper night's sleep will always be a problem for them. Using the analogy of our iceberg what's causing the problems is unseen under the water, not what is visible above it.

Serious depression is a complex multifaceted illness and as such it requires a multifaceted bespoke approach in its treatment. There has never and never will be a one-size-fits-all approach to the treatment of depression because we all suffer it in a multitude of different ways. So unless you have the necessary skill set it is always going to be excruciatingly difficult to treat depression on your own. The problems are compounded by the fact you are trying to use the same exhausted demotivated and irrational thinking mind to get you out of the depression that put you there in the first place.

When someone is at the beginning stages of their journey through depression it is very common for them to treat the early *symptoms* of the illness. The internet is awash with suggestions of taking long walks, being more social, keeping yourself occupied at all times, eating more vegetables or a thousand and one ways to distract yourself from what is really going on. These techniques might indeed work for a short time, and I encourage you to try everything you read about. But, going back to my original point, these techniques are still only treating the symptoms and not the cause. One other downside to consider is this. While you are distracting yourself the depression hasn't gone away. It is working in the background getting deeper and harder to treat.

As with everything in this book, the final choice of whether to reach out for help or not will be up to you and how much of an impact depression is having on your life. Just make sure the choice you make is not based on the fear of appearing weak in the eyes of society. The truth is society doesn't really care what you do. Don't let the fear of what others might think hold you back from helping yourself through this with some help.

Hopefully, I have given you enough information that will now allow you to make an educated decision. I wish you well whatever you decide.

What if depression is my own fault? What if I do it to myself?

Sadly, this is an all too common assumption depressed people make about themselves. Now let me tell you why depressed people commonly make this assumption. As humans, we have an inbuilt *need-to-know* program running in our minds that most of the times we are blissfully unaware of. In other words, there has to be a reason for something/everything to happen. So how does this relate to depression?

When a depressed mind can't find a reason to be depressed it turns in on itself and irrationally comes to the conclusion "If there is no reason, then I must be doing it to myself." Secondly, this irrationality plays into another quirk of the human mind which abhors a vacuum. In the absence of hard evidence the mind will make up a story to fit the context and in this instance, it will hypothesize "It must be my own fault." The depressed person is now caught in a vicious circle between needing to know a reason and the mind making up assumptions both feeding off each other. We all know that all of the above to a rational mind makes no sense, but if you are going through depression all of the above makes perfect sense—such is the nature of the illness. Rational thought can be transformed into irrational thought in the blink of an eye. So how do we counteract this problem if we feel we are caught in this vicious circle?

We need to question our own faulty assumptions. We have to ask ourselves "How *exactly* am I to blame for my own depression, what *exactly* am I supposed to have done to bring me to this place?" Notice I highlighted the word exactly; we want concise answers, not half-truths. If the answer you get back is because someone else told you it was your fault you can discount that immediately. You are the expert on you, not someone else that might have a hidden agenda for telling you that.

Now at this point, you might be telling yourself "I am at fault because I isolated myself or I was anti-social." Let's get something straight. Depression is an illness, not a lifestyle choice; it doesn't enter someone's life because they have chosen introversion over extroversion. Whatever reason you come up with question it, analyze it, and then ask yourself if it is the truth. Better still get someone you know to ask you these questions, someone you can trust to give you an honest answer.

Lastly, if all else fails I have another two questions you could ask yourself that might help put things into perspective. How does blaming yourself help you? How does blaming yourself serve you? I ask you this because you have some hidden belief that needs to be brought out into the open and these questions will do exactly that. At the moment blaming and fault-finding are putting responsibility external to you. These questions place responsibility, and not blame, back where it belongs—with you.

Depression is no one's fault, however, you are responsible for trying to make yourself better, whatever form that may take. Blaming and fault-finding keep us stuck. Put some time into answering those difficult questions and be honest in your answers. Hopefully, it will reveal some blind spots in the thinking you may have. Depression is difficult enough to cope with without pointing the finger of blame at yourself as well. Good luck with it.

Which is the most serious type of depression?

They all are. There isn't a hierarchical scale of depression. If someone suffers 'any' type of diagnosable depression each and every one of them has the potential to bring someone to their knees and in extreme cases take their life.

Every person on the planet will experience depression in their own unique way. What you might regard as petty could be enough to push someone else over the edge into oblivion. Telling someone they will get over it or it's just a phase might be the tiniest nudge they need to make them feel there is no point in continuing.

Most if not all types of depression I have encountered in people come with an extremely deep-seated lack of care about what happens to them. This *not caring* what happens can easily extend to family, friends and just about anything a depressed person holds dear as the person isolates themselves and descends deeper and deeper into an abyss that was not of their making—cutting off the very thing that could potentially make them feel a little bit better.

For someone that has never had to endure their own personal horror movie of depression, they will never know the depths the human mind can sink to no matter how many times it is explained, no matter how many books they read or how many YouTube video's they watch. We literally cannot walk a mile in another person's shoes with depression. We will always be an outsider looking in.

Seriousness is a relative term depending on the mindset and mental health of the person, and if you ever hear someone uttering the word depression in 'any' context it should be taken very seriously. We have no idea what is going on inside someone's head. We are easily blinded by our own stereotypical assumption of how someone with depression should act or behave. We can't see any further than the socially acceptable mask they wear that could be hiding something very serious indeed.

Just so we are clear I am not comparing the likes of seasonal affective disorder to bipolar depression as it is a well-known fact that people with bipolar disorder have a suicide risk of fifteen times that of people with no mood disorder. What I am saying is don't discount the seemingly *minor* types of depression as being of no importance. The feelings of depression can be overwhelming regardless of the type. What might seem trivial to most people can be a soul-crushing experience for another.

As I mentioned earlier a mindset of not caring can be one of the most distressing and serious symptoms of depression. When the person has sunk so low that they care about nothing or no one they start to despair that their life is not worth living. This can very easily transform into losing hope altogether, and when someone loses hope they lose everything with the inevitable outcome.

Is depression an incurable illness?

This question is probably the hardest in the book to answer because there is no definitive answer. It is not a binary choice between yes and no. I personally think the problems arise when we bring the word *cure* into the equation. If someone is cured of something that means whatever the problem was will never return under any circumstances—it is effectively gone forever. There isn't a person on the planet that can give that assurance with any sort of honesty when it comes to depression.

Yes, people can and do get over depression every day of the week. Does that mean for the rest of their lives they will never suffer another period of depression? How could it? We would need to follow that person for the rest of their lives to find out. Someone could be depression-free for twenty years; it still doesn't mean they are cured. It just means they have been depression-free for a period of time and given the right set of circumstances the depression could return tomorrow. The simple fact is if you have suffered depression and are now in remission you are more prone to relapse. That might be a very bitter pill to swallow for some people, unfortunately, that is the reality of this illness.

Next, we have the problem of the word depression itself. When we ask if depression is incurable, which type of depression are we talking about? You already know from reading this book there are ten different types. There is certainly a better chance of coming out of situational/reactive depression than there would be coming out of MDD or bipolar. These latter types of depression need serious treatment by serious professionals. Does that mean they are incurable? I honestly don't know because I would need to have interviewed every person that has ever suffered MDD or bipolar to find out if not even one person has made a full and spontaneous recovery and never relapsed. They are definitely treatable and manageable, but curable is on a whole different level.

Let me give you a personal story about situational/reactive depression which I will probably get roasted for. I am sharing it because I have heard similar stories repeated hundreds if not thousands of times. I had an accident over 25 years ago. For ten of those years, I suffered severe reactive/situational depression as I had lost everything that made life worth living. I also suffered and still suffer constant pain. In theory, once those ten years passed, and I was in remission I shouldn't have suffered depression ever again. The reality is my reactive/situational depression evolved into something very similar to dysthymia which affects me to this day. Why should that be?

My personal belief is that suffering for an extended period of time leaves a mark on the psyche that is not so easily erased. The initial trigger that a person was reacting to with depression might be long gone for instance a divorce, bereavement, loss of a job etc., but the damage has been done, so to speak. I have heard countless stories of people suffering the initial depression only for it to be replaced by a low-grade but persistent and long-lasting depression that can hang around for an awfully long time which leaves them confused. Depression is such a complicated illness that I think the only honest answer one can give to the initial question is . . . maybe. The jury is definitely out.

I've been told I can think my way out of depression, how is that even possible?

The short answer it isn't. I am just going to assume that we are talking about the type of depression that a professional would recognize as such and not a case of the blues or being severely p****d off. In which case, no, you will not think your way out of that type of depression. Why not? Because you are trying to use the same mind that got you into depression in the first place and now that same mind is caught in a whirlwind of negative emotion—it's lost in a maze of powerlessness and despair and needs help. Serious depression requires someone to lead you out of the maze. The question also assumes that there is only one cause for this depressive episode. It takes no account whatsoever of the other types of depression that don't need a cause to enter into someone's life. Let's take a type of depression that does have a cause as an example.

Reactive or situational depression can linger for quite a while after the initial cause has been addressed. The common misunderstanding is that once the initial trigger for the depression is taken care of everything returns to normal, and that is not the case. Let's take a divorce as an example. One would imagine that once the person gets divorced their depression will vanish into thin air. Unfortunately, that takes no account of the self-loathing, hatred, low self-esteem, anger and low confidence that commonly goes along with depression.

The initial trigger might be gone (the divorce) but these damaging emotions can hang around for an awfully long time and potentially cause the person to relapse into depression again and again. Depression isn't a single entity, so to speak; it's made up of a multitude of separate entities that come together to form the complicated jigsaw that is depression. I will use the analogy of a nuclear reactor. The reactor itself can have a meltdown but the fallout and toxicity can remain long after the meltdown has been addressed. That's probably why a very common thing for a depressed person to hear would be "I thought you would be over *that* by now," normally said in a judgmental tone of voice.

Another problem I see with attempting to think our way out of depression is that the mind is locked into a negative spiral. In order to think our way out of depression surely, we would need to be in a positive frame of mind, which is sadly lacking when we are dealing with this illness. Like I said previously, guidance is what is required to navigate the dark passages and corridors of depression. Just thinking about it when we are in a negative frame of mind would be inclined to make things worse, not better.

Lastly, there is a huge misunderstanding surrounding depression in that some people think a depressed person is obsessed with one thought that they replay over and over again and that's what makes them depressed. Certainly, that might have been the initial trigger for their reactive depression but as time passes depression easily descends into an internal battle with self-recrimination and loathing and that's what keeps the depression alive. Can you think your way out of this by yourself? Highly unlikely for all the reasons stated above. Can someone guide you? Absolutely!

When you are severely depressed what are the toughest symptoms to overcome?

They all are because you are trying to use a mind that doesn't want to play ball.

- We want to be happy, but we have lost the ability.

- We absolutely know that *doing things* will help us, but our motivation got up and left along with any energy we had.

- We don't want to push people away, but it feels like we are compelled and have no option.

- We don't want to wear a mask, but we feel we must to avoid social isolation, stigma, prejudice and discrimination.

- We don't want to feel like we are observing our own lives drifting by.

- We don't want to have to go to bed just so we can escape the torment, but it can feel like the only place of sanctuary.

- We don't want to imagine our future with more of the same stretching before us.

Apathy. This is a real killer. A depressed person is fighting a constant battle with themselves. On one hand, they know as a fact that if they could manage to get up and do something it would help considerably. On the other hand, their motivation to actually get up and do that thing is at rock bottom. Unfortunately, the apathy further feeds the depression and can easily transform into a lengthy period of self-loathing which again only serves to feed the depression. They are not stuck between a rock and a hard place as that would imply choice; they can literally feel stuck between a rock and a rock.

Fatigue. There is no doubt whatsoever that fatigue plays a major role in depression. Someone suffering this illness can feel worn down, washed out, burnt out and can feel they are never going to get better. This is further compounded by feelings of helplessness and despair. Their energy levels are at zero and sleep does not replenish.

Isolation. When someone is deep in the throes of depression, they really don't want to be around anyone. Apart from the fact they find great difficulty being sociable and having to wear a mask of respectability they also feel they are being a burden to people. It's a cruel twist of depression in that being social is one of the things that would improve their disposition, but depression makes that feel impossible.

Make no mistake these three symptoms working in conjunction with each other have the ability to paralyze a sufferer into inaction. They feed off each other in a particularly nasty vicious circle. I know many people that have taken to their bed for a week or more. In the severest of cases, I have encountered someone who stayed in bed for six weeks.

If you have never suffered depression and wonder what chronic fatigue and apathy feel like all you have to do is remember what it was like to have the flu, not a cold. Depression is like a flu of the brain minus the runny nose and sneezing times one hundred. At least with the flu you know it won't last. The same cannot be said for depression, and just like the flu, symptoms can include all sorts of chronic pain just to add to the misery. Wouldn't you take to your bed if you felt as bad as that?

How come some people never get depressed?

I have a few issues with this question. There is an implication that *these* people, whoever they are, have found the secret sauce that makes them immune to depression. Maybe there is something about them that allows them to avoid the misery of this illness. This is so not true. There are only three things that can help someone avoid depression and that is dumb luck, coincidence and the law of averages. Depression doesn't much care who you are, what you have or how much positive thinking you do, if it's your turn it's going to happen. That's the grim unvarnished reality.

The second issue I have with this question is, how do we know a person never gets depressed unless we follow them around twenty-four hours a day for the rest of their lives? We can certainly do something we humans are experts at and that is assume that because they happened to be fine when we were in their company for a few hours they must be fine at all other times as well. The truth is someone suffering depression is very unlikely to tell you that they do. They will just pull on their very well-worn socially acceptable mask, smile, and tell you everything is great.

Probably my biggest issue with this question is that I don't really care why other people don't get depressed. My only concern is that you don't use this anomaly as a stick to beat yourself with. It is all too easy to compare ourselves to other people and imagine they must have something special going on that makes them somehow better than us and immune to depression. This sort of mindset can easily lead to thoughts of "There must be something wrong with me," and feelings of not being good enough.

Comparing ourselves to other people when we have no idea what is going on in their lives or behind their socially acceptable mask is a one-way ticket to depression and everything that goes with it. It's only a matter of time before someone would start asking probably two of the most damaging questions to the human psyche: "Why me?" and "What have I done to deserve this?" These two questions have the ability to send the mind on a never-ending journey to try and find an answer that doesn't exist. The mind goes around and around in circles constantly ruminating on these unanswerable questions. Eventually, because no answer is forthcoming there is the very real potential of triggering feelings of being a failure which in turn can trigger resentment, anger and possibly self-loathing. All the ingredients are now in place for a depressive episode to take hold.

The more pro-active and responsible answer to the question of why some people never get depressed should be *it doesn't matter.* All that matters is why you are suffering from depression and what steps you are willing to take to find a way out of it. Even if you could find out why a certain person never gets depressed it would make no difference to you at all because you are not them and you are not living their life. You don't have the same genetic makeup and you don't live in their environment. When we compare ourselves to others and then beat ourselves up it can feel like it might be a way of motivating ourselves to better things. Negative criticism as a motivator never works.

Five very early warning signs of hidden depression

What follows are some very early indicators that someone *may* be at the beginning stages of depression and trying their hardest to hide it from other people. Please be aware that even if the person is displaying all of the symptoms listed it doesn't necessarily mean they are depressed as some physical ailments can mimic the symptoms of depression.

Altered eating habits. Has the person started to eat excessively or maybe the complete opposite and they are eating hardly anything? There is a definite link between eating for comfort and depression. In essence, the person is trying and failing to fill an emotional hole with food which can result in dramatic weight gain. The opposite can also happen, and the person loses their appetite and dramatic weight loss follows. Have you noticed if their weight gain/weight loss has also caused excessive low self-esteem?

Sleep patterns. Has the person started going to bed later and later or maybe they are going to bed during the day because they are tired? Are they getting up in the middle of the night because they can't sleep? Disturbed sleep patterns are a very common symptom of depression. Does the person look generally washed out and complaining that they are getting no benefit from a night's sleep? Sleep deprivation is a very real thing and can contribute greatly to the feelings of depression.

Excessive use of alcohol or drugs. This is an attempt at self-medication that *never* works and usually leads to even bigger problems further down the line when this self-medicating turns into an addiction. Gambling and excessive shopping are another two red flags you should be aware of. All of the above is an attempt at escapism from the crushing feelings depression sufferers experience and should be taken very seriously. Excessive smoking is also a lesser-known form of escapism. Smoking can temporarily alleviate anxiety symptoms that seem to go hand in hand with depression.

Forcing happiness. Another term for hidden depression is smiling depression. We all are very aware of what a genuine smile looks like. Does the person come across like they are faking their happiness for the benefit of other people because it is the socially acceptable thing to do? Have you been able to detect instances of sadness and loneliness behind that painted-on smile? It's very difficult for a depressed person to keep up the pretense of happiness for extended periods of time.

Sudden disinterest in hobbies or friends. Has the person dropped a hobby recently that they were passionate about? Are they telling you they don't see the point to it anymore? The same goes for friends. Have you noticed they are not making the effort to keep in contact with people they know? Are they actively avoiding interaction with these people? They are doing this because they feel that they are going to be found out as it were. They are scared that the people closest to them will be able to see behind their socially acceptable mask. Have you noticed they seem to prefer isolation to integration?

How to help someone with hidden depression

In the previous chapter, I gave you just five early warning signs of hidden depression. Those five signs are probably the most obvious indicators of something that needs to be addressed. There are a few less obvious signs I will talk about before moving on.

Anger and irritability. Most people associate sadness with depression, not anger. However, anger and irritability are quite common. Does the person you know have sudden bursts of anger for no apparent reason? Does that anger not seem appropriate to the situation, is it over the top? Do small things irritate them where previously they would have let them go?

Unexplained pains and aches. Again, most people don't associate physical problems with depression but they are in fact pretty common. Has the person you know started to experience back pain, headaches or digestive problems? Has this started out of the blue for no apparent reason? Are they self-medicating on a regular basis?

If you have noticed these patterns in someone you know the best thing you can do is talk to them about it. This conversation needs to be handled very diplomatically as it can very easily descend into denial and anger especially if the person concerned is not really aware they are performing these behaviors. It is a fact that most people don't realize they have depression until it is brought to their attention by another person—so you need to be tactful. This is definitely not the time to say they need to see a shrink.

The first port of call should be their family doctor where they can get a proper assessment done and maybe discount any physical reasons they should be feeling the way they are. If they are amenable maybe you could make the appointment for them and possibly accompany them to said appointment. This first step is always going to be the hardest as there aren't many people that will happily admit to having a mental health problem—such is the stigma surrounding it. Acceptance is a powerful step to healing.

The important thing is to get them to open up and to keep that conversation going. It is vitally important that you do not become judgmental by asking a question like "What have you got to be depressed about?" If you do this, I can guarantee that the person will start isolating you by not returning calls or texts. They will absolutely find a way to eliminate you from their lives. That's the last thing you want to happen.

The urge to isolate themselves is very strong for a person suffering depression. The best way you can help them is to make sure they stay socialized and interactive with other people. Although exercise is not a cure for depression it is a good way to get someone outside in the fresh air, even if that is only for a short walk if they are up to it. Would you be willing to accompany them on their walk? I strongly urge you not to give a depressed person advice about what they should or shouldn't do as this can very easily become about addressing a need you have. Tactfully make suggestions, place reading matter or leaflets about the treatment of depression in places they can *stumble* across it. Get creative and be supportive; that's all you need to do. The rest is up to them!

Can someone suffering depression be in denial?

I think just about everyone that has suffered depression also suffered a bit of denial at the beginning of their journey. They normally put it down to working too hard, not getting enough sleep, feeling a bit stressed out or maybe they have had some negative event happen in their lives that they can't seem to shake off. This can continue for quite a while as the symptoms become gradually worse and it starts to impact their lives more severely. Even then they are quite commonly saying to themselves *it will pass* given enough time.

Eventually, the person will start doing a little bit of research on depression and maybe take an online test or two. At this point, our depressed person normally does one of two things. They reach out to get help or they start to disbelieve what their own eyes are telling them and go deeper into denial and rationalize that they couldn't be suffering depression because they are strong-minded independent type people that depression would never strike. This mindset keeps them from getting effective treatment as the depression becomes deeper and harder to treat in the background. Many self-medicate with food, alcohol, drugs, shopping and various other coping strategies without connecting the dots and realizing it is the depression driving this.

I would hazard a guess that between the times they realize something is wrong and the person actually turning up at a therapist's office can be as much as two years. It is very easy to convince yourself that depression only happens to other people and not you, it's what we do. This same sort of mindset shows up every day when you sit behind the wheel of a car. Accidents only happen to other people until it happens to you. It allows you to drive a metal box at 70 mph without as much as a second thought.

Culture can play a huge part in the decision whether to seek treatment or not. If you come from a background where mental health issues are frowned upon or disbelieved it will be a lot easier to deny something is wrong than face the stigma, discrimination, prejudice and social isolation that could follow your revelation. You suffering depression in India can be seen as bringing shame on the family with all the consequences that will entail. As an example of this, I read an answer from an Indian physician on an internet forum where he stated that he *hated* depressed people as in his opinion they were weak and not worth the effort. Imagine having that guy as your doctor.

A denial mindset can be particularly strong in men when they have been brought up to believe it is a strength not to show any emotion. This myth is perpetuated by society. It's probably why men are so hesitant to admit to a mental health issue because to do so would be tantamount to admitting defeat and that's something *real* men don't do. These *real* men suppress their emotions only to find they get expressed in a different way like explosive anger. Suppressing emotion is like playing the game whack a mole; you always lose in the end. Can I suggest if you are reading this and thinking "this sounds like me" that you refer back to the chapter detailing the symptoms of depression. There is no such thing as getting treatment too soon.

Why do mornings seem the hardest when a person is dealing with depression?

It is a well-established fact that people who suffer depression, also suffer from disrupted circadian rhythms. The circadian rhythm, or natural body clock, regulates everything from heart rate to body temperature. It also affects energy, thinking, alertness, and mood. These daily rhythms help you keep a stable mood and stay in good health. The illness can wreak havoc on these cycles causing different hormones in the body to go out of sync resulting in something called morning depression.

In essence, these hormones can make someone very irritable and tired when their mind is telling them they should be refreshed after a night's sleep. This can cause a person to feel at a very low ebb indeed. Combine that with the symptoms of depression that are already in place, and you have the perfect storm. Small negative thoughts can take on epic proportions because you have been drained of the will and the motivation to fight back. I will tell you how it was for me in the hope that something resonates with you.

Have you ever seen Groundhog Day?

It's a bit like that without the laughs. There is a time, just a few moments, when you are in that zone between awake and asleep that temporarily your depression can feel like it has gone away. Unfortunately, that moment is very short-lived. As you start to become more awake, and the mind slips into first gear you start to become aware of the dark clouds starting to gather once more. Most depressed people at this point are probably saying to themselves . . .

"Please, not again, can I not just have one day without this torture?" Except their language will be a *lot* more colorful than I just used.

Their bones feel heavy, and they start to experience a mixture of dread and exhaustion as they drag themselves out of bed to battle with the unseen enemy for another day. Sleep is not sleep anymore; it's a temporary escape from the torment of depression. They probably feel as tired now as when they went to bed. They so badly want to have a shower and brush their teeth, but all the time that non-stop voice inside their head is saying, "What's the point?" Can you understand why a lot of depressed people say that they would like to go to sleep and never wake up again? It isn't much fun knowing you have to face this all again tomorrow and the next day with nothing to look forward to but more of the same. I have a few suggestions that you might like to try. The whole idea is to return your circadian rhythm back to normal. These are small adjustments that can have a profound effect. I encourage you to try them.

Try going to bed at the same time every night. Stop taking naps during the day. Avoiding substances that are well known to stimulate rather than calm such as alcohol, tobacco and coffee. Eating at regular times. Not watching television or using a laptop before bed. Sleeping in a dark cool room. Obviously, this is not an exhaustive list, just some suggestions to get you started. If your morning symptoms are severe you might need to consult a doctor for some possible medication.

What are some things a person doesn't realize they are doing when they are depressed? (Part 1)

If you were to ask a depressed person which overriding emotion is commonly present with depression, they would more than likely tell you that guilt is high on the list. A depressed person is all too painfully aware that their house is a mess, that they haven't stayed in touch with friends, that they spend endless hours isolating themselves, that they can at times be very snappy. Of course, they realize they are doing all these things; they just feel powerless to do anything about it. Depression has robbed them of the energy and motivation required to even complete the smallest task. The guilt someone feels when they are stuck in this vortex can be overpowering and only adds to the intensity of the depressive experience.

They one hundred percent know they are overeating, overdrinking, overshopping or overindulging in drugs. What most non-depressed people fail to understand is to a depressed person these strategies seem to work in the short term. All of the above can seem like a pathway out of this torture. Unfortunately, these strategies have a very bad habit of backfiring and making their depression worse as there is very real potential for addiction with all the problems that it brings.

For a non-depressed person that is thinking rationally a solution to all of these problems would be to *force* themselves to take some action, and that's the problem—a depressed person can't *force* themselves to do anything because if they could, they would already be doing it. All of the above is happening at a conscious level, what about some things that are happening just outside of conscious awareness?

Black and white thinking. This can be quite difficult to identify but it usually shows up in a depressed person's way of thinking as "I am either perfect or I am the lowest of the low that deserves to be punished." There are no shades of grey or other possibilities.

Projecting into a bleak future. Depending on the severity of the depression a sufferer will only see the future in terms of not having one. They see a future filled with more of the same mental torture with no possibility of escape. A future is something *other* people have, not them.

Labeling. A depressed person has absolutely no problems labeling themselves as worthless, useless, not fit to live, a burden to everybody, not worth having around and any other negative label you can think of. Unfortunately, a depressed person doesn't realize that the human mind has a nasty habit of looking for evidence to confirm a belief we hold about ourselves—thus reinforcing their own negative view. We can quite literally start acting like our label.

Easily triggered to anger. When someone starts their journey through depression, they probably only get mildly irritated with events and people. As time goes on this irritation can quite easily turn into anger and outright rage at the same event or people. Although rage and depression seem like they shouldn't go together they quite commonly do.

What are some things a person doesn't realize they are doing when they are depressed? (Part 2)

Self-sabotage. This is a very real thing but is mostly confined to people that think they don't deserve to get better. They are punishing themselves for whatever reason. It typically shows up by the person realizing they are starting to get better and then deciding to stop their medication and/or therapy. It's an extremely vicious circle.

Learned helplessness. A person can feel they have tried everything there is to try in an attempt to get better only to find they are confronted with set back after set back. In essence, they feel they can't fight anymore and that it would be easier to just give up, little realizing that this strategy quickly leads to an escalation of symptoms. I have covered learned helplessness in depth in another chapter.

Sarcasm. Maybe I was the only person in the world that used this as a strategy to divert people away from what was *really* going on in my life. At the time I didn't realize I was suffering depression, but in hindsight it was obvious. My vicious sarcasm seemed to appear around the same time. I do remember having to apologize to a lot of people years later and eat a lot of humble pie.

I'm fine. These are probably the two most used words in the vocabulary of a depressed person. It's amazing how quickly this becomes an automatic response if anyone asks a depressed person how they are doing. It's normally combined with the pulling on of a socially acceptable mask to hide a world of pain and allow the person to navigate their life. Depressed people are world-class at hiding suffering.

Not giving a damn. This one might seem pretty obvious, but I want you to think about this for a moment. Have you noticed how not giving a damn has filtered into nearly all aspects of your life? At the beginning, you maybe didn't give a damn about maintaining relationships or giving a damn about yourself. Where are you at now? How far have those tentacles spread unnoticed?

Avoidance. Avoidance can be so subtle you might not even notice you are doing it until someone points it out to you. The sufferer just puts it down to not being in the mood and justifies their reason with logic. Have you stopped calling people or returning calls? How many times have you made appointments only to cancel at the last minute? Have you found ways to not be social? Avoidance is extremely common in depressed people.

Naturally, there will be plenty more examples of things depressed people don't realize they are doing. Depression is a unique subjective experience that is as idiosyncratic as the person suffering it. All of the above doesn't necessarily mean that someone is depressed; it might be just the way they are in life. However, if most things on this list are happening over an extended period of time it might be an idea to get an assessment done with a professional—*especially* if they are out of character for you.

Why don't I even have the energy or want to recover from depression?

This is a lot more common than you might think. Learned helplessness is a process some people go through on their journey through depression. Let me illustrate this point in the form of an analogy.

Imagine you are a keen boxer, and you are getting ready to spar a round or two in the ring. You climb up through the ropes and suddenly you are confronted with the heavyweight champion of the world. This behemoth looks your frame of 150 lbs. up and down, smiles and retreats to their corner. The bell rings and seconds later there are flashes of light, and you feel as if you have been hit by a freight train on the side of the head.

Undeterred you get back on your feet and throw a punch or two in the direction of the train only to get hit again harder than before. This goes on for the next few minutes until you decide it might be better to stay on the floor and not get up. You know that unless the champ is hit by lightning you have no chance of winning. This is learned helplessness. The *fight* against depression has the ability to take every bit of strength and energy you have, and then some.

This is exactly what happens with someone suffering depression. They learn through repetition that it is useless to try and fight something they have no power over. They have read everything there is to read about exercising, positive thinking, eating more vegetables, praying, snapping out of it and every other hair-brained technique to rid themselves of their depression—only to find nothing works. They have decided if nothing works why bother even trying? Go to any depression-related forum on the internet and you will see a myriad of statements along the lines of "I have given up," "I have tried everything and nothing works," "I think it might be time to call a halt to my life," "I am beyond professional help." It is heartbreaking to see these statements as helplessness is a state of mind that can be turned around. Learned helplessness is where the person feels they have come to the end of the road. They feel they have no options, no alternatives and nowhere to turn. They feel they have no other choice than to suffer, and it will be like this for the rest of their lives. Never underestimate the fear of failure as a powerful demotivator when it comes to depression.

But my friend, you are worth more than what depression is telling you. Depression lies to you and that is a fact. I understand it is going to be difficult when you feel you have no energy or will left to fight but fight you must. You absolutely have to get off the floor and try again because the floor is not a good place to be. This time instead of reading about positive thinking, etc. why not enlist the help of a professional to join you in the fight. Together there is every chance you will turn the tables on the champ.

If you are already taking medication, go back and get it reviewed, it might be all that is needed to give you a better fighting chance. If you haven't got a therapist, get one, as medication is only half of the equation when it comes to battling this illness.

If you already have a therapist and they are having no impact, find another one that uses a different approach. Depression is infinitely treatable; it is not an incurable disease. Will it be easy? No, it won't because the lure of the familiar can be a powerful one but has to be preferable to what you are going through at the moment.

People say I am selfish for being depressed, are they correct?

I would be very wary of someone that makes such a statement as generally, they do not have your best interest at heart. Let me explain in a bit more detail. When someone accuses you of being selfish, they are trying to instigate a change in your behavior for their own agenda. What is going unsaid is "I don't like the way you are behaving because it is affecting me in some adverse way." They are using negative or critical motivation to try and effect some change in your behavior to satisfy their own hidden agenda. In effect, they are using guilt as a tool against you to supposedly stop being depressed.

Some people can use this method as a way of trying to get you to *snap out* of the way you are feeling. They have assumed that your depression is only a temporary thing and if they use some tough love, it will resolve the issue. Little do they realize in doing so they have actually made the depressed person feel worse because they are powerless to *just snap out* of their current state. If it was so easy, do they not think the depressed person wouldn't have already done it? It never ceases to amaze me how many people think it is acceptable to try and guilt someone out of a mental health issue. They would never dream of ever saying "you are selfish for having a broken leg" to someone.

Let's explore this a little bit further and have a look at the dictionary definition of selfish.

'Concerned excessively or exclusively with oneself: seeking or concentrating on one's own advantage, pleasure, or well-being without regard for others.'

In my opinion, a depressed person absolutely needs to be concerned about their own well-being. That is not selfish, it is self-preservation. By the very nature of the illness, they are fighting this battle alone. The words excessively and exclusively are irrelevant as they are merely value judgments placed on another person based on their expectation as to how you should behave.

The last piece of the definition, 'seeking or concentrating on one's own advantage, pleasure, or well-being without regard for others' is a complete fallacy when it comes to depression. Depressed people feel like they are a burden to others. How can they feel like a burden unless they have regard for others? It can't be both ways at the same time.

Lastly, I have a little technique you can use if you feel like having a bit of fun with a person accusing you of being selfish. Ask them *why* they think you are being selfish and what it is about your behavior they think is selfish. I can nearly guarantee they will look like a deer caught in the headlights as they won't have thought this far ahead. If you detect they are saying you are selfish because it is somehow affecting them, and they want you to change your behavior, you can turn around and say, "So who is being selfish now?"

Whatever you do never try and justify why you are suffering depression. This is a battle you are going to lose every time because you are trying to convince someone that has the equivalent of their fingers in their ears and going la-la-la-la at the same time.

How to deal with someone that believes depression doesn't exist and doesn't want you to get therapy

There really is no single answer to this question as there are a multitude of different scenarios as to why someone would think this way. The absolute worst thing you could do with someone like this is to go on the attack and demand they believe. All that will happen is you will meet even more resistance as the person goes on the offensive to defend their position. I have a few suggestions that hopefully will help.

Ask questions. You need to be able to open some sort of dialogue with this person. You need to ask *why* they don't believe depression exists. Be aware this person *does* know depression actually exists. Their denial is an attempt to deflect you from the real reason for this statement. By admitting that depression exists they are also admitting that someone they know and maybe love has a mental health issue. Not everyone is going to greet that revelation with open arms. Maybe they don't want you to suffer the stigma, prejudice and possible social isolation that can potentially go along with a diagnosis of depression. Alternatively, maybe they think it will reflect badly on them or the family. There are plenty of countries in the world where that would be the case.

The important thing is to keep asking *why* questions. Just make sure you are doing it in a genuinely sensitive inquisitive way. Asking why questions in a confrontational way will immediately close communication down. You are after answers, not an argument. Remember it takes two people to have a confrontation. Your role is to sensitively tease out some answers, not to score points. This person might have genuine fears that you can allay, it's your job to find out what those fears are and address them. The last thing you want is to make them feel stupid for holding their beliefs. If you feel you have overstepped the mark, it's time to back off. Don't keep trying to ram a point home because it makes you feel better. When you are in a hole stop digging.

The answer to the second part of the question is more or less the same as the answer to the first part. Not wanting you to go to therapy is once again a deflection from what is really going on with them. You need to ask what it is about therapy they are scared of. Do they think it means that you have a serious mental health issue and allowing you to go will confirm their worst fears? There is no doubt whatsoever that a stigma still exists surrounding going to see a therapist. It shouldn't be that way, but it is, and you have to sensitively address that issue which isn't going to be easy depending on the country you currently reside in.

Ask an intermediary. If you can't trust yourself to handle all of the above sensitively, could you ask someone else to do it on your behalf, a trusted relative maybe? Sometimes someone that has no emotional investment in the situation is the best person to act as a go-between, so to speak. Just make sure the person you pick is truly independent—even better if they are on your side. Lastly, you could suggest that both of you make an appointment with your family doctor. Sometimes hearing a professional saying that your depression is very real and that there is nothing to fear from therapy might be enough to get them over the line. I wish you well on your journey.

Is it possible to overcome depression by just reading good books on the subject?

Nothing would give me greater pleasure than to tell you that overcoming depression is as easy as reading some books on the subject. Let me put this into some sort of perspective for you. As you already know from reading the chapter *different types of depression,* there are ten different types. There will also be a scale of severity within those types from mild at one end to suicidal at the other. We also have to take into account that anyone suffering any of those ten types, no matter where they are on the scale, will experience depression in a way that is unique to them and no one else. At the time of writing this book, there are 350 million people worldwide receiving treatment for depression. That's 350 million ways of experiencing this debilitating illness. There isn't a book on the planet that can address so many variations.

Depression would be much easier to treat if everyone experienced it in exactly the same way. Unfortunately, that is not living in reality. Depression cannot and never will respond to a one-size-fits-all approach. The illness really needs to be treated by a professional and that professional needs to have the skill and experience to construct a bespoke treatment plan for their patient tailor-made to their needs. Does that mean you shouldn't read any books on the subject? Not at all. I personally believe it is an excellent idea to be as knowledgeable as you possibly can about what you are dealing with. There are plenty of excellent books out there dealing with the *management* of depression. They are worth reading in case you find something that works for you to make your experience a bit easier. But, if you are serious about finding a resolution to whatever type of depression you are going through, I would strongly urge you to make an appointment with a professional.

Also, try and keep some perspective when reading books by other people that have overcome depression. You will be reading about what worked for *them* at a given time in *their* lives. Realistically, it probably won't work for you given all the variables we have already discussed. Lastly, if you come across any book that offers you some sort of guarantee you would be best served by throwing it in the bin. Absolutely no one can give a guarantee that they can cure *your* depression. If they do, they are either deluded or preying on the vulnerabilities of others to sell books. Avoid this at all costs. If it sounds too good to be true it normally is.

By all means, read books on the subject, just try and keep some sort of perspective as you do and avoid the miracle cure types.

Lastly, a book won't ask the hard questions a therapist will, and a book certainly won't hold you accountable for your answers or guide you to insights of your own. It probably sounds like I am against books, I'm not. What I am against are those books that hold out the false promise of a cure for depression. What normally happens when a depressed person reads these types of books is they try out a few of the techniques and quickly find they don't work. Unfortunately, a depressed person's mind won't assume there is something wrong with the book. It will assume there is something wrong with them, with all the self-hatred/recrimination that goes with it. I don't want that to happen to you. Depression is difficult enough to cope with without adding an extra layer of self-flagellation.

Why don't people believe I am depressed?

There are several reasons this can happen. As a species, we are world-class experts at making assumptions and constructing a story to fit the context, *especially* when there is no evidence to the contrary. It is simply a function of the human mind that goes back countless generations and is in place to protect us, but that's a story for another chapter.

Most people have no experience of depression; they have never suffered it themselves and they probably don't know anyone that has either. Their information has been gleaned from social media and television. They have a stereotypical view of what depression *should* look like and how a person *should* behave. They have a misinformed assumption that someone suffering depression should be curled up in a corner crying all day. Now you come along.

You are wearing your socially acceptable mask and trying your hardest not to let anyone know how much mental pain you are in. You interact with people and might even joke around in an attempt to disguise how you are *actually* feeling. If an observer has a stereotypical view of how you should be looking and behaving, they will put two plus two together and get eight, in other words, you can't be suffering depression because you don't look like you do. Worse still you are probably faking it. Unfortunately, this assumption can be very difficult to overcome because that would be admitting they were wrong. And one thing we humans hate doing is admitting we are wrong, and we will defend our belief despite having zero evidence.

The next reason people don't believe you are depressed is because they don't know how to handle this revelation. In an attempt to rid themselves of the discomfort they are feeling they will resort to denial and trivialization of your very real suffering. There won't be a depressed person on the planet that hasn't heard a version of "don't worry, you will get over it" or "I was depressed myself once and just snapped out of it "or "just think positive and it will go away." Remember these platitudes are an attempt by the person delivering them to make *themselves* feel better, not you.

Another reason why someone doesn't believe you are depressed is for the purposes of their own self-protection. They believe that if they accept you are depressed it will somehow have an impact on their lives and you will become a burden to them. They don't want the responsibility of trying to make you feel better, despite you never having asked. Lastly, there are plenty of people in this world that don't actually care if you are depressed or not. They are so wrapped up in what goes on between their own ears that you barely register as a blip on their radar unless your behavior *directly* affects them.

Have you worked out yet what all the reasons have in common? The common thread is that the other person's hang-ups are the problem, not you. A word of advice: don't make their problem into your problem. Don't let the fact that they can't cope, are in denial or feel the need to be judgmental turn into something that brings you down. Leave the problem where it belongs, with them. You can't be all things to all people. Don't even try as this becomes about a *need* you have. You don't really need any more complications in your life when you are battling depression. I am going to end this chapter with a question for you. Why do you *need* (and it *is* a need) people to believe you are depressed? What is it you want from them? Consider writing down these questions and answering them honestly; you might be amazed at the insights you obtain into your own psyche.

Is going to a therapist like admitting defeat?

To give a sensible answer to this question it would help if we understood what would make someone ask this question in such a way. The answer is societal conditioning. Think about this for a moment. Since we were old enough to understand we have been indoctrinated by our parents, teachers and those we feel have some authority over us that we should never show emotion as it is a sign of weakness and that we are unable to cope. Something others could take advantage of.

We have been told that suffering in silence is somehow an attribute to be admired.

This mindset combined with a concern over *"what others might think of us"* is probably the single biggest obstacle getting in the way of receiving the so desperately needed treatment. Society is a strange sort of creature, isn't it? On the one hand, we are told we shouldn't be ashamed and that we should reach out when we have an issue with our mental health. On the other hand, when we do reach out, we are rewarded with stigmatization and potential discrimination. Go figure.

Here's my opinion on whether going to a therapist is like admitting defeat.

I think it takes a very special person indeed to put their hand up and admit they need help; it takes amazing mental fortitude to then actually do something about it and go against a lifetime of indoctrination and get help. This is a sort of fortitude most of us only dream of. This is the complete opposite of giving in. It gets even more difficult if you are unfortunate to live in a culture where mental health issues are frowned upon and met with social isolation and stigma. The experience of someone suffering depression in India as opposed to the United States couldn't be more different.

I live in an area of the UK where one would think we have a more enlightened attitude to mental health. I have personally found the complete opposite to be true. I have had numerous clients say to me, "I think you have helped me tremendously, but I won't be telling anyone I have been here." I was a well-kept secret, which presents a bit of a problem when you are running a business that depends on word-of-mouth recommendations.

Please, if you are reading this make the call and get the help you probably desperately need. Being proactive about your well-being is a powerful proactive position of self-responsibility. Don't make the mistake of waiting in the vain hope that your depression will go away on its own. This is rarely the case. What commonly happens is the depression gets deeper and lasts longer. If depression is left untreated it has a nasty habit of getting worse, not better. It also gets harder to treat with the passage of time.

It doesn't go away with exercise and positive thinking. It's an illness like any other illness and should be treated as such with intervention by professionals at the earliest possible juncture. Do your mind a favor, make the call. Preferably today.

Which therapies are the best for depression?

There are literally hundreds of different types of therapies available, from the professional end of the scale to the wild and wacky that is best not talked about. What follows is a list of a few of the more generally accepted effective therapies with a specific focus on psychotherapy as it is by far and away the most popular. I encourage you to do your own research into each type as it would require a separate book on each to do them justice. I would also like to add that a particular type of therapy is only as good as the practitioner administering it. A person could have their wall papered with impressive-looking certifications but unless they are patient-focused and have a degree of empathy and understanding they are all but useless. I have met plenty of PhD-qualified practitioners who were more in need of therapy themselves than the people they were supposedly trying to help. I will cover how to find a good practitioner later in the book.

Interpersonal therapy is a short-term treatment. The practitioner helps patients understand underlying interpersonal issues that are problematic: unresolved grief, changes to social or work roles, conflicts with significant others, and problems relating to others. It is a way of learning healthy coping strategies in order to express emotions in ways that improve communication and how we relate to others. It is commonly used to treat depression.

Cognitive Behavioral Therapy (CBT) is based on the notion that how we think directly affects how we feel and behave. Let's say you interpret a situation or event negatively, this will in turn potentially cause you to behave and relate to that event in a dysfunctional way, which can be the first steppingstone on the way to depression and or anxiety. CBT is a way of identifying and challenging these negative patterns so that a person relates differently to them, which in turn can facilitate a change of behavior in the future. I highly recommend the book CBT for Dummies for more in-depth research.

Psychodynamic therapy is based on the concept that behaviors and mental well-being stem from and are influenced by childhood experiences and inappropriate repetitive thoughts or feelings that are unconscious. A patient normally works with a therapist to help improve self-awareness and to change old patterns of behavior and thought to enable a person to experience a more rounded autonomy over their lives.

Psychoanalysis is a more intense version of psychodynamic therapy. It's a system of psychological theory and therapy which aims to treat mental disorders by investigating the interaction of conscious and unconscious elements in the mind and bringing repressed fears and conflicts into the conscious mind by techniques such as dream interpretation and free association.

Other therapies include Dialectical Behavior Therapy, Humanistic/ Experiential Therapy, Person-Centered Therapy and Supportive Therapy. Like I said at the beginning doing your own research is key. These therapies are only as good as the practitioner. No best therapy works for everyone. You might need to try a few of these approaches to find out which is a good fit for you.

How do I find a good therapist?

Let's get something straight right out of the gate. There is no such thing as a universally *good* therapist, only a therapist that's good for you. You will more than likely have to kiss a few frogs before you find your prince or princess. Do a lot of research and expect to ask a lot of questions before you decide who you want to share your innermost secrets with. Finding a therapist that is a good fit for you is a bit like buying a new car. You wouldn't go to the nearest showroom and throw a load of money on the desk and pick the first car you see, would you? The same goes for therapists; don't choose convenience over track record. So here's your first question. Would you rather travel two miles to a convenient therapist or forty miles to a good one?

Do your research. You could start this process by asking people you know that have been to a therapist themselves for help with depression. Would they recommend this person, what was their approach like, did they help resolve their issue, did they find them easy to talk to or did the therapist do all the talking? A personal recommendation can be a good place to start, however, it should not be the endpoint as you still don't know if this person will be a good fit for you. Just because your friend liked them doesn't mean you will.

Ask locally. You could ask at your doctor's treatment center if they have a list of therapists they regularly refer their patients to. This list could prove invaluable as these people will have been vetted and will more than likely have a proven track record. Are there depression organizations or groups in your area? It might be worth a call or a visit to said groups as they will have an in-depth knowledge of what is available in your vicinity and further afield.

Google is your friend. Try googling the word therapist followed by whatever location you live in. You will definitely come across some websites of therapists in your area. Have a good look at them all and also have a look at their reviews. Keep in mind those reviews are still only a snapshot into this therapist and tell you absolutely nothing about what sort of person they are or if you will get along with them. While you are at it check out national databases as well and see if their names come up on them. Check how much they are charging which will give you an idea of the going rate in your area. Keep one thing in mind as you are doing this. If you come across a therapist that is charging considerably more than everyone else do not automatically assume they are better than the rest. They might just want you to *think* they are better than the rest to get your business. Price does not equal quality when it comes to therapy.

Now that you have waded through all the researching you will probably have narrowed the field down to three or four possible candidates you have a gut feeling about. Now is the time to make a few phone calls to get further information by asking a few questions they should have no qualms about answering. Can I suggest you write everything you want to ask down on a piece of paper because I can absolutely guarantee you will forget something important you wanted to ask. Our brains switch into survival mode when we are nervous, and our memory can elude us when we need it the most. Be prepared and you will get the most from your interview.

What questions do I need to ask a potential therapist?

These are just some of the basic questions you could ask your potential therapist:

- Are you licensed to practice? Which professional body are you licensed with?

- How many years have you been in practice?

- What sort of success rate do you have with depression?

- What do you consider to be your area of expertise?

- Which psychological approach do you use?

- What kind of treatments have you found effective in the treatment of depression?

- What do we do if it becomes obvious we are not a good fit for each other?

- Do you offer a free introductory session?

- How long is the waiting list?

- Are there any questions you would like to ask me?

What's important is how they answer these questions, and how they make you feel:

- Are they being evasive and not answering your questions directly?

- Do you feel you are being taken seriously and not being given the brush-off?

- Are they taking their time to answer or do you feel hurried?

- Do you feel confident you are being heard?

- Do they sound knowledgeable?

- Do you feel you are being *sold* to?

- Do they sound genuinely interested in you?

- What is your intuition or gut telling you?

By now you will probably have refined the field down to one or two potential therapists. At this point, you will have to bite the bullet and make an appointment to talk to them face to face. The therapeutic alliance is everything when it comes to therapy. You need to be able to make a connection with the person that will help you through this time. If you don't feel it or they make you feel uncomfortable, it's time to move on to the next therapist on your list. Like I said at the beginning you might have to kiss a few frogs before you find your prince or princess. It is extremely common for people to switch therapists; this is not a reflection on you. Some people you connect with some people you don't.

Lastly, your therapist has seen it all and heard it all before. They will not be shocked by any of your revelations. Don't hold back, ask whatever questions that are on your mind—no matter how trivial you think it might be. If it's important to you it should be important to them. If you feel they are being dismissive, bring it to their attention. Just be yourself and be honest if you want to get the most from your sessions. Remember this important maxim if you want to get the most from your therapy sessions. Therapy is not something that is done *to* you, it is something that is done *with* you, and you are an integral part of the process. The therapist is there to guide you to the answers you have within. They are not there to give you the answers. Happy hunting.

As a depressed person, what is something other people perceive as selfish that is actually a very healthy behavior to practice?

- Some people can see going to a therapist as selfish; they believe incorrectly you must be into yourself. Family is the greatest offenders. They can think you must be selfish because you don't care how it reflects on them that you are seeing a therapist.

- Never ever try and justify a mental health issue you may be having. When you justify you are in effect saying you are sorry for being sick. You don't need to apologize for an illness you had no control over.

- Making and enforcing boundaries. This is a tough one for a lot of people. Friends and family are again the worst offenders. They think by virtue of the fact you are a friend or family they can come and go into your life as they please, and you are selfish if you don't let it happen. Boundaries are very healthy and have to be enforced.

- We teach people how to treat us every minute of every day by our actions or inactions. If you are a doormat, you first had to lie on the floor. Be selfish unless you actually like lying on the floor. Scrutinize people's interactions with you. How are you teaching them to treat you?

- No is a one-word sentence, don't be afraid to use it. Our social conditioning has taught us to not say no. We will beat around the bush and give all sorts of excuses not to use that little word in case we offend and are perceived as being selfish. When's the last time you said NO and meant it?

- Not feeling guilty. To feel selfish you also have to feel guilt and the two are very easily confused. Our societal conditioning has seen to it that we abide by some set of imaginary rules. Who makes these rules? Society makes these rules. Are you not part of society? Did anyone ever ask your opinion?

- Guilt presumes intent. The next time you feel guilty or selfish, stop and ask yourself this question: *What have I done to feel guilty about, have I intentionally done someone harm?* The answer will probably be no. What has actually happened is you have broken one of the BS unwritten rules again. Scrutinize your own actions and do not rely on someone's opinion of you; they could very easily be projecting their insecurities onto you.

- **Admit your mistakes and move on.** Some people believe if you make a mistake, you should be nailed to the wall, and to do anything else is being selfish. You are supposed to atone for mistakes, not move on from them. Moving on from a mistake is healthy; beating yourself up because society says you should is extremely unhealthy.

Educate yourself on societal conditioning. You will be astounded how far-reaching those tentacles go into your life unnoticed. You are doing things right now that you are feeling guilty and selfish for. Examine your life, find out where you are responding to this imaginary book of rules, we call society.

Have you ever thought of examining your relationship with your family and friends to see where you are being silently controlled and manipulated by the use of guilt?

Of course you haven't, you are not supposed to think of your friends and especially your family that way. Says who?

Societal conditioning of course. See what I mean?

What is a good way to overcome procrastination so common with depression?

I have been thinking about this question for a while, or maybe I was procrastinating. Anyhow, I can't think of a better example to give than one I picked from my own life. Hopefully, it will work for you. It's well worth giving it a try.

Procrastination. You do know procrastination doesn't exist, don't you? There are only ever things that get done, and things that don't get done. Procrastination is a label for when there's something we don't want to do. It's an avoidance tactic we employ to sidestep discomfort.

You won't find procrastination listed in any mental health journal, and there are no drugs we can take to help it. It's totally self-generated. When we use this label, we are effectively saying we are a finished project in this area of our life. When we label ourselves a procrastinator, we have very firmly placed ourselves in victim mode and convinced ourselves we are powerless to resist.

Feeling overwhelmed. This normally happens when we feel a project is too big for us to handle. Maybe we don't have the skills or confidence to complete the task. If we procrastinate long enough, maybe someone will come along and complete it for us. We live in a land of hopes and wishes if we think that is going to come true. All this happens subconsciously, of course—we experience the feeling of 'stuckness' and try to justify it with logic.

Procrastination has a nasty habit of generalizing into other areas of our lives. It can creep insidiously into areas where before we never had a problem getting things done. We feel overwhelmed and justify it to ourselves by saying things like "I've become mentally lazy." This label we have given ourselves ensures we now don't have to make an effort.

There is a relatively simple solution to feeling overwhelmed. Divide the task into the smallest components possible and commit to working on those small components on a daily basis.

Some of you may be familiar with this technique, but I've added a twist to make it more effective. It will help to retrain your brain and prevent feeling overwhelmed. Take this book, for example. As this is my third, I knew all too well the difficulties that lay ahead. When I thought of writing it, I could hear my mind trying to talk me out of it. Those subtle little words of *maybe next year* and *remember the last time* whispered to me on a regular basis. Procrastination was around the corner.

What is a good way to overcome procrastination so common with depression? (Part 2)

So what did I do? I kept my mind in the here and now, and not projecting off into a future where all I would experience would be feeling overwhelmed. I divided the project into small pieces and reckoned if I wrote five hundred words per day, and took an enforced break at the weekends, I would have the book complete in about six months.

So I started writing five hundred words per day which in time seemed to naturally increase to one thousand a day, and sometimes as many as fifteen hundred. I kept total focus on the job of writing those words. Once I'd completed my quota, I stopped. I resisted the temptation to keep going because I knew it would become boring, and that's a very similar feeling to procrastination. The getting started bit was important. Once I was committed, everything else fell into place.

You can do exactly the same with something you're holding back from doing. Divide the task into small doable pieces and focus intently on one small piece to the exclusion of everything else. Once you have this piece done, stop. Rinse and repeat the next day. Forget about the big picture for the moment. Focus on what's in front of you.

I'll now give you a technique to help keep your mind focused on the here and now, although you will have to adapt this to suit your particular project.

The whole point of this process is to keep your mind focused intently on the task at hand. You want to stop your mind from projecting into the future and triggering procrastination. How? By focusing intently on the process of whatever it is you're doing.

In my case, this meant concentrating on the act of doing rather than the end result. If my mind started to wander, I simply brought it back to the here and now by focusing on the keyboard as I typed. I could feel the touch of the keys on the tips of my fingers. At times I became intently aware of my breathing. This kept my mind in the present. If it wandered again, I did the same again. The periods of wandering became shorter the more I practiced. I was training my mind to stay in the present.

You would be amazed how much you can get done by implementing this technique.

It's important you resist the temptation to continue, no matter how good it would feel to do so. Stop, and don't work on your project again until the next allotted time slot. This could be at the end of the day or even the next day. Only you can decide what is best for you. You'll be surprised how much you can get done and how quickly the time passes. When you're focusing on the here and now, time becomes an irrelevance. Once you've completed your small task, it's important to walk away from it and do something unrelated. This is called a *pattern interrupt*. Have a coffee or go for a walk. It doesn't really matter what you do as long as you do something different. The method I've described is designed to work with your mind in the way it likes to work. Your mind likes nothing better than short bursts of intense concentration. So why not work with it the way it was designed to work?

Do depressed people only have themselves to blame?

I want you to find a large paintbrush and a bucket of paint. Now, go outside and paint on the side of your house I AM NOT TO BLAME, NOT NOW, NOT EVER. I can completely understand why an individual with depression might think this way as the illness can cause someone to think in very irrational ways indeed. But this particular thought simply isn't true in any way, shape or form. Depression *happens* to a person; they don't go out and invite it in.

Blame implies fault. How can it possibly be your fault that an illness entered your life and decided to take up residence in your brain?

I hear a counter-argument to this all the time. Someone that doesn't know what depression does to a person might comment "Well, they are depressed because they isolate themselves, are anti-social, hate themselves (fill in the blank)." What they fail to realize is that all of the above are *symptoms* of depression, not the cause. They are merely observing the external manifestation of an internal problem. People can be very quick to make judgments even if they have zero evidence to back their judgment up.

People like things neat, tidy and pigeonholed. It's so much easier to criticize than to try and understand. So much easier to point the finger than look in the mirror and admit they might be wrong because they are not in full possession of the facts. Therefore, if they don't understand what caused your depression, they will assume you caused it yourself? Sad but true.

If you are unfortunate enough to encounter one of these *it must be your fault* types, ask them to tell you exactly *how* it is your fault.

They won't have thought that far ahead and you can enjoy watching them squirm. Just remember not to let them palm you off with a symptom, isolating, etc., as the cause of your depression. That just about covers other people blaming you for your depression. What if it is you blaming yourself for the illness? Would you blame yourself if you developed migraines or epilepsy? Would you blame yourself if a car mounted the pavement and hit you breaking both of your legs? If you don't blame yourself for those scenarios which are out of your control, why would you choose to believe you are to blame for your depression? I can tell you why.

From a very young age, we have been indoctrinated to believe that if we just try hard enough, we can overcome anything, and that if we can't overcome adversity we are either weak or a failure, maybe both. If we have problems we can't cope with it must be down to a lack of willpower or internal fortitude. So you can easily see why someone might think the problem lies within themselves if that is what they were brought up to believe. It's a myth, a societal construct you have chosen to believe.

The downside of believing this myth is that it prevents people from accessing effective treatment because of the fear of stigma. They swallow their suffering and pretend everything is fine and hope it will go away on its own—it rarely does, it only gets worse. Maybe it's time to let go of this outdated not fit-for-purpose belief. Don't fall into the trap of thinking beliefs are set in stone and unchangeable. You are *choosing* to hang on to this belief. Maybe it's time you chose a better one?

Will positive thinking cure my depression?

Ah, the old *just think positive* chestnut once again. On a superficial level, it can seem like a reasonable idea that to cure negativity all we need is positivity. I want you to take part in a little experiment with me that should put this fallacy to bed once and for all. You will be closing your eyes for a minute or two so find somewhere safe that you can do so.

Once you close your eyes, I want you to picture someone you don't particularly like. Imagine what they look like, the sound of their voice, anything in fact that brings clearly to your mind why you don't like them. Keep that image front and center for about one minute. If you are doing this correctly it will probably trigger feelings of anger, resentment or maybe even a need for revenge. Now, after you have completed your one minute, I want you to do the opposite. This time I want you to think positive thoughts about this person for another one minute, observe what it feels like and then open your eyes.

Did you notice that your mind kept trying to drag you back to the negativity . . . why is that? Your mind has a history of negativity associated with this person stored in your memory. It knows absolutely when you are trying to think positive about this person that it is not the truth. It knows you are trying to shoehorn something into the psyche in an attempt to override the predominant emotion you have for this person. It rejects the positive and reminds you of the reality of the relationship you *actually* have. It does this to protect you from harm, but that's a chapter for another time. It's why we find it so hard to forgive someone that has wronged us. We have to work very hard to overcome the protection mechanism that is located in a very primitive part of our brain.

Now, let's replace someone you dislike and imagine you are replacing dislike with chronic depression that has extremely well-established neural pathways already in place and you can understand why positive thinking for depression doesn't work. The depressed mind can eliminate a positive thought in the blink of an eye. It can just as easily turn a seemingly positive event into a negative one. Positive thinking against depression is merely a distraction that cannot be maintained. It can certainly give someone a temporary lift in the moment but sadly that moment will be very fleeting as the negative neural pathways once again establish control.

Positive thinking can potentially temporarily alleviate some of the symptoms of depression, but it cannot and will never address the depression itself. We need to get to the root of why the depression is there in the first place, not gloss over it. Let me give you an analogy that might help give you some perspective. You are the pilot of an airplane and all of a sudden, all the alarms start going off with red lights flashing everywhere. Would you turn off all the alarms and think to yourself "I'm so glad those alarms were there" or would you investigate what caused the alarms to go off in the first place?

Depression is the same. Positive thinking without addressing the root cause of the depression and then committing to positive action is like flying the plane with the alarms switched off until the inevitable happens.

What are some of the lesser-known effects of depression?

I can only answer with my own personal experience on this one; although I think quite a few people will empathize.

When I think back about how depression affected me when it was at its worst, I can vividly remember long periods when nothing seemed to go my way; literally everything I touched seemed to turn to mud. If King Midas could turn everything into gold, I managed to turn everything into mud. It was more than likely just a coincidence but man it caused a great deal of stress and depression at the time.

It just seemed to be one bad thing happening to me after another and another and another; if it hadn't had been for bad luck I would have had no luck at all. Damaging my car, losing money, losing friends and a thousand and one other things that just kept happening usually within a short period of time. On their own, these things would be relatively minor, but when it happens in conjunction with a severe depressive episode it can easily feel like the straw that broke the camel's back.

I found out up close and personal that saying "it can't get any worse" was a fantasy as it inevitably did get worse, a lot worse. I found out rock bottom had a basement and another and another. I think sometimes people think when they hit rock bottom that somehow it will give them a solid surface to push off from on the road to recovery. I have rarely found this to be the case. I have found the exact opposite to be true in that the person is so exhausted when they reach rock bottom, they have no strength left and their *rock bottom* turns out to be mud that they get stuck in.

Of course, I know now that it was all about my state of mind and not the universe out to get me, but at the time it felt very personal, and that the universe *was* out to get me. I literally could not catch a break, or so it seemed. This seemed to happen for months at a time. I think that was the biggest challenge for me. That feeling of being out of control and unable to influence what was happening. Being scared to try *anything* in case it too turned to mud and made me feel even worse. A sense of autonomy is extremely important to human beings. In other words, we like to feel as if we have some sort of control over our lives. Those periods felt like the complete opposite. It seemed to feel like I had no choice other than to put up and shut up.

If you have experienced this *put up and shut up* feeling you will know it feels like you are trapped—unable to make choices or decisions in case they have a bad outcome and made matters worse instead of better. So you rationalize that it would be better to make no choice at all. Ironically, when you choose not to choose you are actually making a choice. You are choosing to sit on the fence where it appears to be safer. Sitting on the fence is seldom a good idea as it comes with its own unique sort of pain.

It definitely seemed at that time like being stuck between a rock and a rock. Damned if you do, damned if you don't. It felt a bit like standing on the top of a 100-meter flagpole that was at the edge of a cliff that had a 1,000 meter drop. A very scary place to be.

How do I respond when someone asks "What have you got to be depressed about?"

I am going to suggest something that has the potential to irritate you but stay with me and I will explain my counter-intuitive suggestion. When you are confronted with this question there are two possible ways to respond to it that will ensure you don't end up having to defend your position. You could choose to remain silent, or you could state something that is true by saying "I don't know."

If you do anything else you will just end up trying to defend, explain, justify or worse still trying to convince the other person you are the real deal when it comes to depression. You don't need to defend, explain, justify or convince anyone about anything concerning your depression. I make no apology for repeating that message that you have probably read several times already; the message is so important. Now, let's explore this question a little further. I want you to wonder why someone would ask such a question. I can only think of two reasons. The person asking the question is making a genuine inquiry about your welfare or they are attempting to trivialize your very real suffering. In the vast majority of cases, it is probably the latter as someone that knows you well wouldn't need to ask you such a question in such an accusatory tone. It will be up to you to decide what the position of the person asking the question is and act accordingly.

If you know them well and you know they care for you an appropriate response would be "I don't know, and that is what is so frustrating." At the very least this can open a dialogue between the two of you. Just ensure when that dialogue is opened that you don't use it as an opportunity to unload everything that is wrong in your life unto them. They are not your therapist and in doing so you run the very real risk of closing them down and becoming unable to support you. Tread carefully! Have a conversation, not a therapy session no matter how tempting it is. The truth is you probably don't know why you are suffering depression especially if you haven't consulted with a mental health professional. There are quite a few different types of depression and quite a few of those don't need a reason to show up in your life. Someone suffering reactive or situational depression can usually pinpoint the reason it started. That's not the case with other types of depression.

Now, let's talk about the person who deliberately is trivializing your situation by asking that question. The best answer to a person like this is to actually say nothing and just shrug your shoulders. This sends a powerful two-pronged message; you don't know why you are depressed, and you don't want to talk about it. If they persist you could simply state "I don't want to talk about it." The object of the exercise is to shut them down, not take part in a game of defending yourself that you are not going to win. If you get into a dialogue with this person, you will regret it as they will have a counter-argument for every reason you put forward. I completely understand that you want to retaliate your ego has a need to put someone straight when slighted but don't waste your time.

What should you say to some that says "Why don't depressed people just do something and try and change?"

Their question implies that depressed people do nothing to help themselves when in actual fact the polar opposite is true. They are battling with their own mind hour by exhausting hour trying to reason and rationalize their way out of this personal horror movie. If they aren't doing that they are pulling on a socially acceptable mask and fake smile so they can navigate their world, their jobs, their relationships—everything in fact that most people take for granted and which make life worth living.

If they aren't doing that, they are having a daily battle with people that think a platitude is a substitute for care and understanding. On top of that, they have to listen to other people's unsolicited opinions about how they should get out of their depression and all this coming from someone that has never suffered it. Gems like "why don't you do something and try and change" are what depressed people have to tolerate on a daily basis. It makes you wonder why they never thought of it themselves.

On top of all that, and probably the worst thing of all, they have to live with the constant fear that they are going to be trapped like this for the rest of their lives living a non-life while they observe the rest of the world go by. They have to watch as their life crumbles before their eyes—powerless to do anything about it.

I have never met a depressed person that isn't constantly looking for a way out of this torture. Books, the internet, therapy and medication; we have tried it all. Sometimes we hit on the right answer, sometimes we don't. Depression consumes a person's life. They have to suffer it and try and find a way out of it at the same time. That's a 24-hour a day job that leaves them exhausted, demotivated and even more depressed.

So when someone says "Just do something and just try and change?" I would love to hear their suggestions. And if they reply with do some exercise, eat vegetables, trust in the Lord, think positive, snap out of it or be more sociable, tell them we have heard and tried it all only to find out it doesn't work.

Depression isn't a lifestyle choice. For many, it can be a life-changing/life-ending illness.

Depending on my mood at the time I might try and equate depression with something in their own lives they could relate to. I would ask them why they phone the helpline when their computer isn't working. They phone because they don't know what to do apart from staring at a blank screen in the hope everything will resolve itself.

The human mind is like that, it doesn't come with an instruction manual on how to get out of a serious mental health issue like depression using the same exhausted demotivated mind that caused the depression in the first place. A professional can help but it can take a lot of time and effort to put those shattered pieces back together again. We can't simply turn ourselves off and back on again to reboot our mind.

What do I say to people that don't believe I am depressed?

I want you to write this down and place it somewhere as a constant reminder. If privacy is an issue repeat this as many times as it takes for the message to sink in.

"You don't need to explain, convince, defend, justify or make excuses about anything to do with your depression to anybody."

If you do you will fall into the same trap that thousands before you have fallen into, and that is trying to convince people you are the real deal when it comes to depression. This becomes about a *need* for validation you have and is a one-way ticket to even more misery. Think of it this way if you have a *need* to try and convince people of your illness it won't be long before you start either doubting yourself or get very angry and frustrated—both of which you don't need at this time.

You are looking for something they can't give you. They can't give you value.

It is not your job to educate people and in doing so you are ensuring that this strategy will backfire on you dramatically; it is your job to get better and not waste your precious time on people that do not want to be educated. You have to understand when someone says "I don't think you are depressed" they are giving you an opinion based on their own ignorance and misunderstanding and they are going to defend their position vigorously. They haven't the first clue what depression can do to a person unless they have gone through it themselves, so try and take their *opinion* with a pinch of salt. Do you really want to get into a debate with such a person?

I understand completely the need to retaliate. The ego does not like being put down, but when faced with this scenario you are better off biting your tongue and moving on as you will be fighting a losing battle. Let them think whatever they want, as long as you know the truth that's all that matters.

Think about this for a moment, if you try and justify, defend or convince someone you are in essence apologizing for being ill. Why do you need to apologize for something that by and large is out of your control? You didn't wake up one morning and decide to be depressed for a few years. You have enough to deal with without engaging in this nonsense.

There is one last alternative you could try depending on the relationship you have with the person you are talking to. Hand them a copy of this book as they are precisely the audience it was intended for.

You could do that, or you could just grow a slightly thicker skin and understand this is just their opinion and they are coming from a position of misunderstanding. Of course, you will always meet people that will make the statement in an attempt to make themselves feel better by putting you down in a judgmental manner. Honestly, it wouldn't warrant the time to write about these types.

If at all possible, get them out of your life as quickly as you possibly can.

Can relationships suffer because of depression?

Absolutely they can. When someone is suffering depression a very common thing for them to do is isolate themselves away from other people. They do this for several reasons. Some do it because it requires so much energy that they haven't got to communicate and be sociable while at the same time wearing a socially acceptable mask and pretending everything is fine.

Some people do it because they believe they are being a burden to other people, and some others are just plain exhausted from the daily battle with their internal struggles. Obviously, if you are in any sort of relationship with someone that performs either of these behaviors, especially isolation, it will put a huge strain on the relationship. Everyone has a limit to the amount of exclusion they will put up with. That is why divorce is reasonably common in married couples where one of them is suffering depression.

Friends will only accept being stood up for appointments so many times. People soon tire of being ignored and disappointed. Another aspect of depression is negativity. It takes a very strong person indeed to let the negativity commonly displayed by someone with depression wash over them with no ill effects. If someone is faced with negativity on a daily basis it won't be long before they decide they would rather not be in your company.

Depression is a bit like a hand grenade going off in a metal room that contains all the people you know—the closer they are to you the more they are going to get hurt.

If you are the person reading this that suffers depression you are well acquainted with black and white, all or nothing thinking. I am going to suggest you try and change that mindset, even slightly. Even a daily five-minute phone call to someone you know can help alleviate the extreme loneliness that comes from isolation, it also keeps lines of communication open with people that you are going to need in the future. A five-minute walk can break the cycle of staring at four walls or sleeping so that you can escape the torture of your own mind.

Make no mistake I know how excruciatingly difficult this will be for you to summon up enough motivation to complete these small tasks. Please, for the sake of your own sanity give it a go.

If on the other hand you are reading this and you know someone suffering depression, please allow me to give you some valuable advice. Never try and force, humiliate, criticize or guilt someone into doing something they really don't want to do. Always let the depressed person take the lead despite the temptation to use tough love in the thought you are helping them, you aren't, you are making matters worse for them. Negative motivation never works.

If you continue with negative motivation don't be surprised if you find yourself being an ex-friend/partner very quickly. The very best thing you can do is be supportive and try to understand what they must be going through. Life isn't easy when you feel hopeless.

Do some people not want to get better?

I couldn't blame you if after reading this question you were thinking "this guy has lost his mind, why would anyone in the world want to suffer the misery of depression out of choice?" And to a rational thinking mind that would be a fair question to ask. Here's the problem. A depressed mind doesn't think rationally, irrationality makes perfect sense for the depressed mind. That's why people with depression commonly isolate themselves from other people when actually being social is the very thing that could help them. This is the sort of conflict depressed people have to deal with on a daily basis. Never underestimate the power irrationality has over someone suffering depression.

Now, let's get back to the question *do some people not want to get better?* Strange as it may seem, yes, some people don't want to get better. Not because they enjoy the misery but because they believe they deserve to be punished for actions or inactions in their past. I want to give you an example of this kind of self-punishment. But before I do I what you to understand behavior does not exist in a vacuum; we all do things for a reason. We might not be consciously aware of the reason, but it exists nonetheless. Keep this in mind as you read on.

Paul was a client of mine and had already been to see two other therapists. He had situational/reactive depression and had thwarted all attempts at getting better from medication to working with mental health professionals. He came to me thinking he would give this therapy thing one more go and that was it.

To cut a very long story short it transpired that Paul had bought his son a motorbike which the son subsequently crashed and was killed. Paul was a broken man but still resisted all attempts to help him move on. It turns out Paul was punishing himself for buying the son the motorbike as to his irrational depressed brain he *should* have known what could happen. Obviously, there is no way he could have known what could happen.

His depressed brain rationalized that if he got better, he would be betraying the memory of his dead son. In effect, Paul believed he deserved to be punished for the rest of his life because of this one mistake, which in turn fed his depression. What happened to Paul? After a *lot* of work, he was able to let go of the self-flagellation and move on with his life. He came to realize that his actions instead of respecting his son's memory were actually doing the complete opposite. We, humans, are complex creatures. Most of the time what you see is not what you get.

We are past masters at presenting a socially acceptable mask to the world while inside we are suffering a world of pain. Never make the assumption that when someone says they are fine that they actually are. If this chapter resonated with you on any level and you are justifying not getting treatment by telling yourself it doesn't work, you might want to explore the reasoning behind that. Write down all the reasons you tell yourself not to get help . . . maybe you are like Paul and punishing yourself. If so, you really need to reach out and get help as soon as possible.

Can meditation, exercise and positive thinking cure depression?

There is nothing that would give me greater pleasure than to tell you all of the above cure depression. The harsh truth is they don't, but they can be an effective temporary relief from the symptoms. I am assuming when I am writing this chapter that we are talking about the type of depression a professional would recognize and not just a case of the severe blues. Let's take each of these practices and examine why they might not be a solution to your depression.

Before we start, I would like to point out that any practice that alleviates the horrors of depression is a great idea. Meditation and exercise are great for managing depression, but they are not a cure. I will come on to positive thinking later in the chapter.

Meditation. Meditation, whether you suffer from depression or not, is a great habit to get into and one I would strongly recommend. I would certainly urge you to do a *lot* of research into the various techniques and schools of thought. The biggest mistake newbies to meditation make is just closing their eyes and thinking because that's what it looks like the meditator is doing. Nothing could be further from the truth. If you would like to get into meditation you could do no better than researching mindfulness meditation by Jon Kabat Zinn. YouTube has numerous videos and lectures to help get you started. Meditation can be a great way to manage depression (not cure) if done correctly. If done incorrectly it can exacerbate symptoms.

Exercise. The feel-good chemicals released into the brain during exercise have been well documented. There is no doubt whatsoever that exercise helps a depressed brain to some extent. Unfortunately, because we can't exercise 24 hours a day the effects by their very nature are short-lived. I have read on countless occasions that exercise is the panacea for depression. I can only imagine the authors of these claims have never suffered the horrors of full-blown clinical/bipolar/or major depressive disorder where the sufferer can barely function much less motivate themselves to exercise. With exercise think management rather than cure. I am absolutely suggesting giving it a go, just try and keep things in perspective.

Positive thinking. Anyone that has suffered severe depression will quite categorically tell you that positive thinking has zero effect. Feelings of hopelessness, worthlessness, powerlessness and desperation will not be diminished by positive thinking. The depressed brain isn't stupid; it knows exactly what you are doing when you engage in this activity. It absolutely knows your positive thoughts aren't true, it knows you are trying to shoehorn something into the psyche it doesn't believe and will reject every attempt. Just think positive is a platitude that depressed people are sick of hearing as it comes across (and is sometimes meant) as a trivialization of a person's very real suffering. By all means, give it a go; just try not to be disappointed when it doesn't work. Try everything you can to alleviate suffering but remember these shouldn't take the place of professional treatment as you are allowing the depression to deepen and thus making it harder to treat effectively.

Can depression make your world smaller?

It certainly can if you let it. Depression by its very nature is an intensely personal experience that is completely unique to the person suffering it. One thing that all types of depression have in common is a need to isolate. The person will deliberately isolate themselves away from other people in an attempt to gain some sort of control over their situation. Ironically it is the complete opposite of what they should be doing as isolation only serves to feed and reinforce the depression.

I think if you speak to most people that have suffered depression there seems to be a word that crops up time and time again and that is loneliness. The sufferer feels so alone because no one understands what they are going through no matter how many times they try to explain it. In essence, they are correct as no one can understand how another person feels. Even if someone has suffered depression themselves, they can never know what it is like for the other person. Naturally, this feeling of not being understood combined with loneliness can promote feelings of being apart and different from other people. It can seem like the world is closing in on them. Strange as it may seem a sufferer can feel profoundly alone even when surrounded by people they know and love.

Self-isolation is very common in depressed people; they push people away and retreat into their internal world with only their own dark thoughts for company. As you can imagine once someone reduces their contact with the outside world their own world shrinks considerably. They find it next to impossible to put in the effort required to maintain friendships and relationships. It's easier to not bother than it is to make the monumental effort required on their part. This effort requires energy they simply don't have as it has been depleted battling their depression on an hourly basis.

Isolation is absolutely guaranteed to make a sufferer's world smaller as other people will eventually give up trying to help. It takes a very mentally strong person indeed to keep showing up for a depressed person when they are constantly met with rejection, missed appointments and sometimes resentment. Once friendships dissolve and relationships break down the depression sufferer's world can become microscopic.

Another common reason depressed people can isolate themselves is because they feel they are being a burden to others and that they bring people down with their negativity. This is an extremely difficult mindset to shift even for a seasoned professional—such is the complexity of this illness.

I would like to finish this chapter on a purely personal note that is coming from someone that suffered this dreadful illness for ten years. If at all possible, try and maintain your friendships and relationships no matter how difficult it is for you because other people can bring much-needed relief from the miseries of isolation. I am not suggesting you need to go partying, just lift the phone now and again and have a five-minute conversation. Believe me, this is going to be difficult, but not half as difficult as it will be if you let these relationships slide and end up with no one to talk to or confide in.

Why did my depression turn into anger?

Depression is a seriously complicated mental health issue. It can express itself in a myriad of ways, one of those ways being anger. A person can start off with prolonged episodes of anger which can easily transform into depression given enough time. Anger can be a sign of needs going unmet. Depression can be the next step if those needs remain unmet as their resentment is internalized. Another complicated way anger can show up in depression is as follows. The person starts off with depression, the anger makes its presence felt and then the person goes back to being depressed again. Let's take our first example and examine it a bit more closely.

Let's say someone has lost their job and they spend their days sending out applications only to get rejection letters back. You can easily see how this would make someone angry as they rail against the unfairness of their situation. Eventually, they start to lose hope of ever finding a job. That hopelessness can easily transform into helplessness and further transform into feelings of worthlessness. They see their inability to get a job as a direct reflection of who they are as a person. All the ingredients are now in place for depression to take hold. They are reacting to their predicament and can very easily end up with something called reactive depression which is unlikely to improve until their situation improves.

Now let's look at our second example and examine what's going on there. This person is already suffering depression and they are doing a reasonable job at suppressing the negative emotion that goes with it. This person could also have a great deal of self-hate. They hate themselves because they believe they are weak for not being able to rid themselves of their depression. They feel they *should* know what to do and they *should* be able to eliminate it from their lives.

This emotional flagellation builds and builds until the inevitable happens. They explode in anger because suppressed emotion will *always* find a way to express itself; it comes back wearing different shoes, so to speak.

It started off as depression, it turned itself into a barrage of self-hatred and resentment, and then back again to depression. Because self-hatred and resentment are so corrosive once the outburst is over the person will quickly return to being depressed again, until the next time. This pattern can continue for years if left untreated. It's a particularly vicious circle.

One last thing before we leave this chapter. I would like to mention something not particularly related to anger, and that is the feelings of grief and loss people sometimes experience with their depression. Why is that? It's really no surprise when someone suffering depression feels that part of them has died. They are mourning that part of their identity that makes them . . . them. They can experience a profound sense of loss if they feel that part is never coming back. They can feel resigned to their fate which in turn feeds the depression. Yet another vicious circle. If anything in this chapter has resonated with you, can I suggest you consider counseling? It is incredibly difficult to unravel this on your own. Reach out for some help.

Why do other people not want to talk about depression?

Unfortunately, as a society, we have not reached the point that it's as easy to talk about mental issues as it is to talk about what was on television last night. Mental health is still very much a taboo subject for an awful lot of people. Should it be that way? No, it shouldn't but wishing it so won't make it a reality. It's something we have to deal with. When we bring up the subject of our own mental health we will *generally* be shut down for a variety of reasons by other people. Not all the time of course.

We make the other person uncomfortable. The vast majority of people that we encounter have zero experience of serious depression. They haven't the first inkling of the horrors inflicted on a person suffering this illness. Think of it this way, when most people hear the word depression, they probably think the person is a bit sad or feeling a bit down, they certainly won't be thinking along the lines of a serious mental health issue. Then we come along and start using words like *in the depths of despair* or maybe *feeling like we are at the bottom of a very dark deep hole unable to escape.* We will certainly trigger feelings of discomfort in this person as we have shattered their preconceived notion of what depression *actually* is. We have pushed them way out of their comfort zone, and they will be looking to find a way back to it. In an attempt to minimize the discomfort they will minimize the experience of the sufferer. If I had a dollar for every time someone said "Don't worry it will pass," I would be living it up somewhere in the Caribbean on my yacht.

They don't want to get involved. If you talk to someone about your depression and you intuitively know they are backing away from the conversation it could be because they feel you are going to be hard work or a burden. They can feel it's simply not worth their investment in time and energy to try and make you feel better, despite never having been asked for their help. They can feel that somehow your depression is going to negatively impact their lives. This type of mindset speaks volumes about the person you are talking to. Their shallowness knows no bounds and you should avoid them whenever possible.

Some people don't care. I know this can be a particularly bitter pill to swallow especially if it is family, but the reality is that unless we *directly* affect someone with our behavior we barely register as a blip on their radar. People are so caught up with their own problems they don't want to add your problems to their ever-expanding list. It's very common for depressed people to have their experience diminished or trivialized by someone that doesn't care. It's all too common for a sufferer to hear the words "what have you got to be depressed about?" uttered in an extremely judgmental tone. The question is not designed to elicit information; it's designed to close the other person down. I hate to say this but there is very little advice I can give on how to deal with these three types of people apart from avoiding them or growing a thicker skin. Whatever you do, don't fall into the trap of trying to convince them you are the real deal. They aren't listening. If you persist, that becomes about a *need* you have for validation. Don't go there! Depression is difficult enough to deal with without more added complexity.

Why would someone say depression is just a phase?

There are various reasons why someone might make this statement. You will have to use your own judgment to decide which applies to your particular set of circumstances.

They want to make you feel better. Sometimes people can deliberately minimize your experience in an attempt to make you feel like there is light at the end of the tunnel, so to speak. It's a way of helping the depressed person feel they are going to get through this, and it won't last forever. Whether what they are saying is true is another matter entirely as they have no way of predicting your future. It feels true to them.

To make themselves feel better. These types of people have no actual interest in whether you get better or not. Their motivation is to make *themselves* feel better because they have been confronted by something that makes them feel uncomfortable. They do this by issuing a platitude that on the surface seems helpful but actually has nothing behind it. Saying *just a phase* is a way of trivializing the very real suffering of the person on the receiving end of this platitude. In their mind *just a phase* means unimportant. They have effectively reduced a person's experience to something as unimportant as the common cold.

Misunderstanding. Depression is a seriously misunderstood illness. Most people you know have never experienced depression themselves, and more than likely they know of nobody else that has suffered serious depression. To them, depression means you are just sad. This is something they have experienced themselves and they know from experience that sadness passes. Because they believe that depression is *just sadness,* they also believe this sadness has a time limit aspect to it. A phase is just another word for a period of time when they assume the sadness/depression should cease to exist. It's very common to hear such people say, "Are you *still* depressed?"

Avoidance of reality. This happens quite often to young teens. They tell their parents they are depressed only to be met with a denial of their experience. They are assuming that if they minimize their experience it will somehow magically disappear. This can have a seriously detrimental effect on the person concerned. They won't see this as a denial of reality. They will process this as a person who supposedly is there to protect them who doesn't care about their suffering. It is certainly true that *some* teens do go through a period of what seems like depression, but some are not all. Better to err on the side of caution and get things checked out considering teen suicides are on the increase. Don't gamble with someone else's mental health.

A way of inflicting hurt. The reality is there are people out there that will reduce, diminish and trivialize your suffering as a means of deliberately hurting you. What motivates someone to do this is beyond the scope of this book as it is an entirely separate mental health issue of its own. It ticks a mental box in their psyche when they can be harshly judgmental toward their fellow human beings. I doubt if they even know the reason why they do it. If you can, avoid such people like the plague. You have nothing to gain by engaging with them because primarily they couldn't care less about your suffering.

Why would someone with depression commit suicide?

Before we get into this question in any depth there are a few facts I think you should be aware of. The vast majority of people that suffer depression do not go on to commit suicide. Yes, the severity and longevity of a person's depression put them at greater risk than the average person but that still doesn't mean the numbers are huge. Just so we are clear I am not saying those people that sadly do go on to commit suicide are inconsequential or insignificant. The ending of a human life for whatever reason is a tragedy.

I think if we consume social media or television news, we can easily be fooled into thinking the numbers are higher than they *actually* are as they attempt to sensationalize the suffering of others. It's a sad reflection of our society that bad news sells. If it's celebrity bad news, so much the better.

Something else we need to consider. Probably every person that has ever suffered depression has at one time or another wished they were dead. I certainly have and anyone I have talked to has thought the same. It's a very normal part of the process and at times is used to blow off steam, so to speak. Wishing you were dead is not the same as actually doing something about it. It is however something that should be addressed with a professional especially if you have reached the stage of planning how to do it. This is called suicidal ideation and should be taken extremely seriously.

Hopelessness. I think for most human beings once they have lost hope it can certainly feel like they have lost everything. When someone feels they have lost all hope and they feel powerless to change the situation it can very easily overshadow anything they might consider positive in their lives. While it can appear to an outsider that things will improve or get better, to a depressed person pessimism and despair that are common with the illness can blind them to the truth of their situation or circumstances. They quite literally cannot see how their situation will ever improve.

Physical pain or illness. As someone that has suffered physical pain because of an accident for the last twenty-five years, I can attest to the fact that at times it is extremely difficult to live with. As a former swimming teacher and someone that had a keen interest in bodybuilding, it can be very difficult to have your life restricted to such a point that you feel like a burden to others. Pain comes quite high up the list as a reason some people go on to commit suicide. It's not easy living with something you absolutely know is never going to change no matter what you do.

Cry for help. Sometimes people attempt suicide not because they actually want to die. They do it as a way of reaching out to other people when they can't explain in words how much they are suffering. It is not merely a way of getting attention and should be taken extremely seriously because most people that make a second attempt at ending it all succeed. If any of the above has affected you please talk to a professional or call the suicide prevention line in your country. You will find some suicide hotline numbers in the back of this book. You are not alone and there are people willing and able to help.

Why do I feel like I am faking my depression?

To understand why this is so it would be helpful to understand how the mind works and the role it plays. The mind has an unbelievable capacity to adapt to whatever harsh circumstances it finds itself having to deal with. There's even a name for it, it's called *hedonic adaptation*, which is just a fancy way of saying it gets used to what is happening in the environment.

A great example of this would be the horrors that some people endured in concentration camps during WW2. They had the threat of death and violence hanging over them on a daily basis. Amazingly some people survived to tell their story of how they adapted in these death camps. I would urge you to read *Man's Search for Meaning* by Viktor Frankl who survived the harrowing experience and went on to practice as a psychotherapist helping fellow survivors after the war. I digress.

I want you to think back to the worst days at the beginning of your depression. Now, compare how you felt then to how you are today. In *most* cases hopefully, there will be a difference. Your depression is exactly the same—it hasn't gone away; you are not faking it. What has changed is that you have adapted to the circumstances you find yourself in and your depression can feel *not as bad*. Unfortunately, at this point, some people are fooled into believing they are on the road to recovery and so they stop taking their medication and cease therapy. Then the inevitable happens. They find out their depression is all too real.

They have what they would call a relapse when in actual fact it isn't a relapse; it's a continuation of what they were suffering that has surfaced again because they have stopped their medication and/ or therapy.

Apart from hedonic adaptation, there is a secondary more pernicious reason someone might imagine they are faking their depression and that is the attitude of other misinformed people. If you are told daily that you should *just snap out of it or just think positive thoughts and asked "is it really that bad?"* would it really come as a surprise if someone started doubting themselves and feelings of faking it started to creep in? Let me put it this way, if I told you on a daily basis that you had a big nose, how long do you think it would be before you started checking it out in the mirror? It's the same thing.

A major trap a depressed person can fall into when they hear these platitudes is looking for validation from these people that they are the *real deal* when it comes to depression. Unfortunately, this strategy won't work, and never will as they are trying to convince someone that is deaf to their suffering and doesn't really care that much either. If this looking for validation continues it's a surefire way to convince yourself you are faking it. Some people in their ignorance have a stereotypical idea of how a depressed person *should* look and act. If you are not curled up in a corner crying you must be faking it. Stop trying to educate the misinformed about your depression as they are undeserving of your time. Concentrate on trying to get better and let them go on their ignorant way whistling a happy tune. You don't need to justify yourself to anyone.

Why do I joke around when depressed?

It's a coping strategy. Some people use alcohol, some people use drugs, and some people use shopping—you use humor. There are normally three reasons why someone uses humor to cope which I will address in a moment. First, I would like to address an implication in the question that might not be immediately obvious.

There is an implication in this question that if someone jokes around, they are not suffering 'real' depression. Nothing could be further from the truth. We need only think of Robin Williams as someone that joked around professionally, yet they felt their depression was real enough that it compelled them to take their own life. We can never assume when someone says they are *fine* that they actually are. We never know what is going on in someone else's life. We are all masters at disguising pain and suffering from the outside world.

Now, let's get into the reasons someone might joke around when depressed.

It makes them feel better. They say laughter is the best medicine. I don't know how true that is for all mental health issues, but it can certainly lift the mood of someone that is depressed, albeit temporarily. There can be no doubt that laughter releases the feel-good chemical of serotonin/dopamine into the brain. When we are laughing or making other people laugh it can be a welcome distraction from the misery that is depression. It's free and won't harm your body, so why not? Just keep in mind that just because you can laugh it doesn't mean you are faking your depression.

It is used to disguise pain and suffering. Humor is a great way of distracting other people away from the fact that we are suffering deeply. The vast majority of depression sufferers are experts at subterfuge and distraction because they don't want other people judging them, criticizing them or possibly socially isolating them. The stigma of a mental health issue is very real. They have become experts at presenting a socially acceptable façade to the world as doing the opposite has real-world consequences. They are so good in fact that when they take someone into their confidence about their illness the normal response they get is "I never knew, you always seemed so happy."

High-functioning depression. As the term implies some people can have depression and still function to a degree. Does that mean their depression isn't real? No, it means they have found a way to function in their world while still suffering the miseries of depression. It doesn't make their suffering any less *real* than anyone else's. Unfortunately, because of the stereotypical image most people have of depression where they think someone depressed should be lying in bed crying all day, these people are the most likely to suffer prejudice, discrimination and stigmatization. They are the people most likely to be thought of as *faking* their depression for sympathy and attention. Isn't it ironic that society tells us we should not be afraid to speak up about our mental health but when we do or display a behavior that doesn't fall into the stereotypical norm we are met with the very real potential of all of the above?

I feel empty, I never feel satisfaction in anything, and I don't understand why. I'm not depressed because I don't feel sadness. What does it mean?

This is a very common error.

It's very easy to make an assumption that depression equals sadness; it doesn't. Depression is a lot more complex than just feeling sad all the time. Depression is more about emptiness than sadness. This wrong assumption could potentially hold someone back from perhaps getting some help. There is possibly another wrong assumption at play here as well. This person could assume that material things are supposed to bring them happiness, only to find out they don't.

As a species, we have an inbuilt striving mechanism that has ensured our evolution through countless generations. Today that striving mechanism is still in place. However, these days we are not striving for survival we are striving for the next shiny object that we assume will somehow make our life complete. We assume that getting that new car, new house, new job, new husband/wife or more money will fill that emotional void we are feeling. We are chasing an endpoint that doesn't exist in reality as we compare ourselves to other people and imagine the wonderful life they must have. A comfortable life does equal a happy or contented life.

Social media actively promotes this feeling of not being good enough with some people basing their worth as a human being on how many likes they get. It seems to me if you are popular on social media, you are *somebody* and if you are not you don't exist. I personally find this a very strange and damaging phenomenon as nowadays someone can be famous for doing nothing more than uploading photos of their pretentious life to a media platform. Yet someone that actually has done something with their life gets vilified on the same platform. Go figure.

There could be yet another dynamic at play here that the person might not even be aware of and that is something about their upbringing. If they weren't allowed to express emotion (or feel they couldn't) in childhood and maybe adolescence it can have a very real damaging effect in adulthood. Repressed emotions will *always* find a way to express themselves. With some people, the repression is projected outwards in the form of anger and rage. With others, it can be turned inwards and the repression shows up as a profound feeling of emptiness. We are all different and can experience this in a myriad of different ways—anger and or emptiness being the most common.

Our mind abhors a vacuum and as humans, we are experts at trying to fill this emotional void. Alcohol, drugs, sex, gambling, shopping, overeating, you name it, and someone has tried it. These strategies all have one thing in common, they don't work. They provide an emotional lift in the moment but as a long-term solution, they are doomed to failure and can generate bigger problems in the future in the form of addiction and or obsessive-compulsive behaviors. These forms of self-medication are *always* an indicator of something more serious going on below the surface. Our minds crave familiarity and consistency even if we know the behavior is causing us damage; ask any smoker or alcoholic. It can keep us locked in this spiral of damaging behavior unless we somehow break the pattern. The mind doesn't really care whether something is good or bad for us it only cares about repetition.

In the question the person states they don't know why they are feeling this way. Would it not be a good idea to talk to a professional who can help them understand? What have they got to lose by talking to a counselor or a therapist to obtain a deeper understanding of their emptiness?

Can I cure chronic depression naturally?

The first thing I would say to someone asking this question would be to drop the word *cure* as the word cure implies that their depression will never return under any circumstances or for any reason in the future. At the moment there isn't even a cure for the common cold much less one for something as complicated and subjective as depression. Depression can certainly be effectively treated, but *cure* is not a word I feel comfortable using because currently there is nothing available that cures all ten different types of depression that works for all people, permanently. Now, let's explore the question further.

The person has used the word chronic in the question so this would imply that their depression has been around for quite a while and isn't simply a case of the blues or being fed up. I am going to make an assumption the person has self-diagnosed themselves with reactive or situational depression. I am doing this because the more severe forms of depression like bipolar would have required serious treatment a long time before it ever got chronic. That being the case it is *highly unlikely* a natural remedy would have any impact on their long-term depression.

Chronic or persistent reactive/situational depression requires professional treatment. It also requires that the root cause of the problem be addressed otherwise it is destined to return given the right set of circumstances. A natural remedy might help someone feel temporarily better, but all it is addressing are the symptoms of depression and not the cause. It is the equivalent of using a band-aid on a gaping wound. Think of depression as a bit like having an abscess in the tooth. You can treat it with antibiotics by yourself, but eventually, you are going to have to visit a dentist to address the root cause.

I can completely understand why someone might want to go the natural route as a potential way of getting them out of the mire they currently find themselves in. It can seem quite attractive to be able to buy something across the counter at your local health food store and not have to tell anyone how you are feeling or divulge what you perceive to be your darkest secrets. I want you to keep one thing in mind. Depression is a *medical* condition and the longer you experiment with your mental health the deeper and more resistant to treatment it can become. Time is literally of the essence when it comes to this illness.

If you are still not convinced and are determined to go the natural route, I would like to make a suggestion. Why not combine the natural remedy of your choice with some form of talk therapy, that way you will have the best of both worlds, so to speak? Your natural remedy will be addressing the symptoms while the talk therapy addresses the cause.

Notice I have not been as prescriptive to state that natural remedies don't work, however, the evidence for their effectiveness as a stand-alone intervention is weak. There will be people that swear by natural intervention. Personally, I am not an advocate. At least now you have enough information to make an informed decision.

Now I have overcome depression, how do I deal with the fact that I have had that time stolen from me? I could have done so many things.

Obviously, this chapter is aimed at those fortunate people that have come out the other side of depression but are still left with the nagging feeling that they need to do something about the time they perceived to have wasted when they were depressed. Don't skip this chapter because you think it doesn't apply to you as I will be talking about acceptance which plays a huge role in the recovery from this illness.

I used to do exactly what the question alludes to until I realized that it was keeping me trapped in the past and what *could* have been. I realized I was wearing my past like some sort of emblem that I wanted everyone to see and understand how bad it was for me how much I had suffered. The only problem was, nobody noticed, and nobody cared.

Once I finally was free of depression, I went on to replace that emblem with another one. I had replaced my badge of depression with another badge—one of a lost past.

I finally got off that hamster wheel of misery once I could accept that what had happened, happened and there was nothing I could do about it. Does that mean it was right? No, it doesn't? Does that mean I was happy about it? No, it doesn't? Does that mean it was easy? No, it wasn't? Was this a way of erasing the past and pretending it didn't happen? No, it wasn't, it was the complete opposite. It was a way of facing the reality of the past and moving on despite the familiar pull of wanting to put the past right.

People can see acceptance as akin to *put up and shut up or feeling like a doormat.* That isn't acceptance; that's grudging resignation. Acceptance is understanding that the past is unchangeable and no amount of wishing the opposite is going to make any difference, it happened and is now part of your personal history. At this point, I want to ask you a question. What would you be giving up if you decided acceptance was the way to go? The need to show people how wounded you are. The need to constantly ruminate about what *could* have been. You would be giving up nothing positive, that's for sure. How would your life look if you never had to carry this burden again?

The past is a great place to visit but you really don't want to live there.

I sincerely hope that you can get past this and embrace acceptance because there is real potential here for you to go down the path of "why me?" "life's not fair" and "what have I done to deserve this time getting taken away from me?" if you don't. It's very difficult to move forward if you are constantly looking over your shoulder in anger at what could have been and wondering how to change your history.

You are an amazing person for having come out the other side of depression. Don't throw it all away because of a story that you are creating about the past. You don't need me to tell you what the next stage of that mindset will be. Try not to see acceptance as being a failure. It's the complete opposite; it's a sign of maturity and strength.

What did depression teach me?

Two things spring to mind; one good, one not so good, and depending on how far along you are on your own personal journey the first might come as a bit of a jolt. I always said I would be honest with you. Depression will teach you that you will get out of it exactly the same way you got into it, *on your own*. Yes, there will be people that will help you along the way like medical professionals and hopefully family and friends but in essence, you will find this is one journey you will take by yourself.

The good thing about taking this journey yourself is that it puts you in control of your own destiny; you are not depending on someone swooping in and putting things right because that is never going to happen. You and you alone assume responsibility for your own well-being. That's a very powerful position to be in assuming you are willing to take that responsibility as it ensures you do not take the position of victim to this illness.

I know from bitter experience how easy it is to point the finger of blame at other people, events, and the world. You name it; someone with depression has blamed it. Unfortunately, as a strategy for recovery, it will never work. Once you point the finger of blame you have unwittingly ensured you stay stuck seemingly powerless to fight against something outside of you. Taking self-responsibility (not blame) and being proactive eliminates feelings of being like a victim against the unseen monster.

How do you get proactive? You never stop looking for something that can help you. I have detailed at the end of this book how I got out of depression, but it required an awful lot of hard work to get there. There will be setbacks and failures along the way that is the nature of the illness. You will have to make an effort when you would rather just pull the covers over your head and go back to sleep. At times it can very much feel like one step forward and two steps back. But that doesn't mean you don't start.

But, here's the thing, you have this. You have coped with your illness up to now otherwise, you wouldn't be reading this book. You have been coping all your life, you will cope with this, and you will get through it. One positive thing that ten years of depression gave me was the ability to cope with anything that life has to throw my way in the future. I found that when I thought I had hit rock bottom that rock bottom actually had a basement and another and another. I still clawed my way back and coped, and you can too!

Today the internet can literally be a lifesaver; we have so much information at our fingertips. I can guarantee that however bad it has been for you someone else has had it worse and wrote about it. Reach out, get proactive, find out how they got through, use this valuable resource to its fullest and hopefully, you will find something that resonates with you. I understand completely how difficult it is for you. Even if you only spend five minutes per day reaching out, it is five minutes closer to getting out of this pit of despair.

Can being a perfectionist cause depression?

It can, because striving for perfection sets up a conflict in the human mind that it can't resolve because perfection doesn't exist. It's an ego-driven perception that bears no resemblance to reality. We are trying to attain something that will forever remain out of reach which can very easily lead to anxiety and depression. It's a mind game of smoke and mirrors that has no resolution.

There is a very easy way to determine if perfection *actually* exists in the real world. All we need to do is ask ourselves a few simple questions. Who measures perfection? It obviously can't be ourselves because we are not perfect. So how can we possibly know we have reached perfection when there is no possible way of measuring it? We can't rely on someone else's judgment either because they would need to be perfect themselves—where did *they* get the authority? Can you see how this can lead us down a very deep rabbit hole?

Secondly, if we make a mistake at any time in our pursuit of perfection does that mean we are no longer perfect? Considering that humans learn by their mistakes we can only come to one conclusion, we are not perfect; no one is. We are a constant unfolding work in progress. Striving for perfection seems like a worthy pursuit, doesn't it? Unfortunately, the human mind can have other ideas when it comes to chasing the unobtainable.

Let me explain what happens in the early stages of our quest for perfection. Everything can seemingly go quite well for a period of time; we reach a goal and then just like a pole vaulter we raise the bar a little. We continue this process of reaching goals and raising the bar, each time working harder and harder to obtain results. We work harder and harder because that is what has worked in the past, right? Then the inevitable happens . . . we can't clear the bar of our self-imposed target.

At this point, the self-criticism starts. The would-be perfectionist is judgmental in the extreme with themselves because they think that negative motivation will help them to clear that bar. It won't. They assume that they are feeling so bad about themselves because it must be an indication they are not trying hard enough, never realizing they are feeling so bad because they are chasing something that doesn't exist in the real world. Something has to give, and it will always be us.

This pattern continues until the ego starts to become involved and the self-talk at this point will be along the lines of "you're not good enough," "you are a failure and if you just tried hard enough you could be perfect." You don't need me to tell you that once this starts happening, you are on a fast track to anxiety and depression. The feeling of not being good enough strikes to our very core at an identity level; we can easily accept this belief as if it were *actually* true. I strongly urge you that if you are chasing the illusion of perfection to stop before it transforms into something altogether unexpected. You can be good, very good and maybe even brilliant. You will never be perfect. You are not giving up on a dream, more like preventing a nightmare from occurring.

Can someone else cure my depression?

Unfortunately, asking this type of question is similar to asking "can someone else cure my broken leg?" There will be people that will put your leg into a plaster cast and maybe give you some painkillers but ultimately it will be your own body that will do the healing. Depression is no different. There will be people that will help you with medication and therapy but ultimately you will be the one doing the healing; it is 100% down to you. It really can't be any other way as abdicating responsibility to another person for your mental well-being is destined to fail. You absolutely can come out of depression; people are doing it all the time. How long will it take for you? There is no way to predict that. Some people can go into remission fairly quickly, however, for some, it can require time and patience. It also requires a mindset that you are not your depression, it does not define you as a person unless you identify with it, it is part of you; it is not who you are. Depression and you are not one and the same.

The first thing I would urge you to do is to stop using the word *cure* as it implies that your depression is gone forever never to return under any circumstances. If anyone gives you that sort of guarantee they are either deluded or not in possession of the full facts as to how the illness functions. Depression is way too complex and multifaceted to conform to a one-size-fits-all approach. Everybody suffers in their own unique way.

For instance, when you hear someone state they got out of depression by doing *XYZ* in all likelihood their *XYZ* will not work for you. They are telling you what worked for them at that time. By all means, I encourage you to try everything from A-Z, just try and keep some perspective when you do. The cause of your depression is unique to you, what triggers it is unique to you, and so will your path out of it. Medication and/or therapy can help ease the symptoms and maybe give you the strength to continue the battle toward remission—they are not a cure. These are choices only you can make.

With regard to therapy in particular it is not a panacea; it requires you to do a lot of hard work at times when you feel you would rather not. The therapist's job is to encourage you to do the work; they can't do it for you. Therapy and medication do not cure depression; they do however vastly increase the chances of you finding a way out of this emotional turmoil. Lastly, in the majority of cases where people suffer depression, there will be times the depression lifts for a period of time. I strongly urge you to use these times productively. Do your research, read books, attend online seminars, do anything that increases your knowledge. Find out everything you can about it. Find out how other people got out of their depression. More importantly, put your knowledge to use by trying everything you are learning about . . . who knows you might stumble across something that works perfectly for you. Don't sit around dreading the arrival of your next episode or worse still taking online depression tests, do something! Use these windows of opportunity to increase your chances of getting better. I hope you find the strength to come out the other side. I for one will be rooting for you.

Can comparing ourselves to others cause depression?

Comparing ourselves to others doesn't lead directly to depression. Instead, it insidiously eats away at our self-esteem resulting in a feeling of not being *good enough* which in turn has the potential to lead to depression. It can also lead to feelings of frustration, anger, resentment and disappointment. Let me explain.

If we feel the need to compare ourselves to others, we are subtly telling ourselves we are not good enough. So when that happens our mind starts to become involved, and not in a good way. It will start telling us if we were slightly more attractive, had more money, a better house, a better car we would feel fulfilled. So let's say by some miracle we managed to achieve all of the above, what do you think will happen next?

Once again, the mind will become involved, and we will start off on the comparisons treadmill once again and dissatisfaction will start to set in. Just like a pole vaulter, we will raise the bar of our expectations each time until ultimately, we fail. Now the mind will start telling us we couldn't clear the bar because we are not good enough, smart enough, and never enough. As you can imagine with all this going on in the mind it doesn't take many more steps to lead to depression as our needs are going unmet.

Comparing ourselves to others is a mind game that can never be won as ultimately, we would have to be perfect in order for us to be better than everyone else, and as perfection doesn't exist, we are starting on a journey that has no endpoint. We will never be satisfied because our mind thinks that perfection *does* exist and if we can't reach it, it's because we are weak. People often fool themselves into thinking that if they compare themselves to others, it motivates them to bigger and better things. In the extreme short time that might in fact be true, but just like our pole vaulter we are ultimately destined to fail.

Does that mean we shouldn't even try? No, it doesn't. By all means, be the best *you* can be if that's what you want, just don't use comparing yourself to others as a vehicle for getting there. Something else for you to consider. When we compare ourselves to others what are we actually comparing? We have no idea what goes on in someone else's life. We *all* wear a socially acceptable mask depending on the context we find ourselves in. We *all* project a version of ourselves we want others to see. How do you know the person you aspire to be isn't in the depths of despair and depression? They are hardly likely to tell you, are they?

If you read the above statement and thought to yourself "I don't wear a socially acceptable mask, what you see is what you get." Really? So you are exactly the same with your boss as you are with your Mother and vice versa? You do wear a socially acceptable mask, you just don't realize you are doing it. Lastly, you are a unique individual, be the best you want to be, however that looks to you. Look for your validation internally, be your own cheerleading squad. Forget trying to be a pale imitation of someone else because at best you are going to fail and at worst you are storing up a potential mental health issue in the future.

Should I give a depressed person advice?

That depends. Are you qualified to give advice on a mental health issue? Do you actually know what you are talking about? Have you suffered depression yourself and therefore feel qualified to give advice? Have you actually been asked for your advice? Unless you are a qualified mental health professional, I would say you shouldn't give a depressed person advice, and that includes advice from someone that has suffered depression themselves. Why? It's very easy to do more harm than good.

All depression is not created equal, what you went through will never be experienced the same as what the person is going through at the moment. The best advice a former depression sufferer can give to someone suffering at the moment is to get in touch with a mental health professional as quickly as possible.

Depression seems to be one of those things that everyone seems to have an opinion and advice on despite the fact they have never suffered it themselves. Unfortunately, they don't realize they are not dispensing advice they are dispensing platitude to make themselves feel better in the moment and these platitudes can cause real harm. Things like "just think positive," "eat more green vegetables," "go for long walks," and my personal favorite "just snap out of it" are not advice.

When you say these things to a depressed person, they are not thinking to themselves "Wow, why didn't I think of that?" They are thinking "depression seems so easy to get out of according to this person so there must be something wrong with me if I can't." I personally think there is something even more damaging than this and it's when a seriously depressed person opens up to someone about their illness only to be greeted with "Oh, I was depressed myself once and just gave myself a good shake and got out of it."

There is absolutely nothing to be gained by making a comparison of what you went through to a serious mental health issue. It's degrading for the person on the receiving end to have their pain and suffering dismissed and trivialized so easily. It has the effect of making the person regret opening up in the first place, which in turn feeds their depression. If you feel the urge to give advice about depression, ask yourself two questions. Has the person actually asked for my advice? If I give them this advice, is it designed to make them feel better or me feel better? Put yourself in their shoes for a moment and think through how your advice is going to be received. Someone that has been seriously depressed for more than two months has heard every piece of advice and platitude ever uttered. Do you have something original and helpful to say or are you giving advice because it *seems* the right thing to do? Nine times out of ten they have heard it before.

Great advice for someone suffering depression is "I know the name of a great therapist. Would you like their phone number?" "I heard XYZ treatment is very helpful in resolving depression, would you like me to do some research for you?" Think long and hard before giving advice, you could inadvertently be doing more harm than good.

What positives could depression add to my life?

This was actually quite a difficult chapter for me to write. On the one hand, I didn't want to credit depression with adding anything to my life except for misery; on the other hand, you are reading a book about depression *exactly* because I suffered it. It's a bit sweet and sour, to be honest. What follows is my own personal take on the subject; I understand completely that your experience might be the polar opposite.

Empathy. Suffering ten years of depression gave me the ability to see the same in others. It doesn't matter how much they try to disguise it; I can see it as clearly as if I was looking through a window. Unfortunately, it can at times be a bit of a double-edged sword. On the one hand, I am able to help them through their journey with depression but on the other hand, I am acutely aware of the pain and feelings of hopelessness they are experiencing. Empathy probably drove me to want to become a therapist. It is certainly a great ability to possess if you are dealing with other people's raw emotions.

Self-awareness. Depression has taught me that I need to be acutely aware of my own negative self-talk. If I choose to ignore the signals it might take me down a path I don't want to go and lead me into a depressive state. If you want to cultivate your own self-awareness, I can highly recommend mindfulness meditation. It only takes 10–15 minutes per day, no sitting cross-legged, no chanting and there are numerous different types for you to try until you find a method that resonates with you. This self-awareness has also taught me to meet problems head on rather than ignoring them in the hope they go away—they won't.

Independence. I have learned from bitter experience that when you suffer depression it's a very lonely place to be. There isn't another person on the planet that will understand what you are going through as depression is an intensely unique experience for the individual. Friends that you have known for years can disappear overnight when they are subjected to a barrage of negativity, even family can react in some weird and wonderful ways you would not have expected. Depression will educate you that when the going gets tough the only person you can absolutely depend on is yourself. Of course, some people will help you along the way, just don't become dependent on them.

So that's the few positives I can say that depression gave me. Make no mistake those positives were not in place as I went through my own battle. They showed up sometime later. Like I said at the beginning I find it very difficult to credit depression with anything, I had to pay a very heavy price for empathy, self-awareness and independence to show up in my life. I sincerely hope your experience is completely different.

I have started to recover but some of my friends seem resentful

Strange, isn't it? We would assume that people we know would be happy for us that we are improving. Instead, in some cases, the opposite can be true. Let me break down this issue a little bit further so you can get some perspective on it. First and foremost, I need you to understand something very important. Those other people are the problem, not you.

When we make *any* changes in our lives, we unwittingly change the status quo or dynamics of any relationship we happen to be in. Whether that is friends, family, work colleagues or whoever, they are going to be affected to some degree by our decision to change. Think of change like dropping a stone into a pond, the ripples spread out in all directions. Resentment from other people is usually a sign we are doing something that is making them feel uncomfortable because we are holding a mirror up to their own behaviors and they don't like it. Think about what is happening here for a moment.

This person would like you to remain depressed, anxious, stressed or whatever to fulfill a need *they* have. They might have seen themselves in the role of rescuer, fixer, confidant or a shoulder to cry on, and now you have taken that away. In extreme cases, this is known as a co-dependent relationship. One person assumes the role of rescuer and fixer while the other person assumes the role of someone that needs rescuing and fixing. I digress. Think of your friends, family, work colleagues, etc. as a little private gang, metaphorically speaking. We all know our place within the gang, and we all follow a set of unwritten rules. We have expectations of them, and they expect certain behaviors from us. Then we decide to change.

What normally happens in this scenario is that *some* members of our metaphorical gang will try to undermine us and our attempts at change in an attempt to maintain homeostasis and consistency. You have probably experienced this yourself if you have ever tried to quit smoking or tried to lose weight. I don't think many of us haven't heard the words "one more won't hurt" or "you don't need to lose weight, you look great the way you are." Make no mistake this is undermining in action.

What motivates someone to undermine another's efforts can probably find its roots in jealousy, envy or resentment that they are unable or unwilling to make changes themselves, even more so if the other person is suffering depression. With depression, they say that misery loves company. That's true as long as they both stay the same.

Keep a careful eye on those that would undermine you as they haven't got your best interest at heart. Their reason for *only trying to help* is to remove their own discomfort. Unfortunately, as much as we would like the opposite to be true, when we instigate change there will always be some collateral damage and some relationships may have to be reassessed; it comes with the territory. Not everybody will be happy to join us on our journey to whatever goal we have in mind. Try not to take it personally. Ask yourself, "Is this person helping me to move forward or are they holding me back?" You will intuitively know who has your best interest at heart and then act accordingly.

Can holding a grudge cause depression?

I am not going to give you a direct answer to this question. Instead, I will lay out the case about grudges and you can decide for yourself. If you have got this far in the book you will already know the answer. First, I want you to partake in a little experiment with me; it should only take a minute or two.

I want you to vividly remember the person or persons you have the grudge against. Visualize what they look like and how they sounded, it should be very easy as you have been doing this for quite some time. Notice that feeling in your body of anger and resentment and whatever else comes to mind. Notice what you would like to say to them and the venom in your voice. Keep doing that for about a minute or so.

After the minute has passed, I want you to ask yourself this question: "What has changed?" Did the person/persons you hold the grudge against feel your anger and resentment or did you just let them victimize you all over again? When you berated yourself, which you most certainly did, for not standing up for yourself who felt that pain in their body? Was it you? Of course, it was. So my next question to you would be if they are totally unaware of your anger and resentment and totally unaware of your self-hatred who is getting hurt by this behavior? You are the *only* one getting hurt.

At this point, you might be tempted to say to yourself, "If I stop holding the grudge it means they have gotten away with it and it feels like I am forgiving them." That's a story you are telling yourself. The reality is they have already gotten away with whatever *it* was and that is not going to change even if you hold this grudge for the rest of your life. As far as forgiveness is concerned the people that wronged you neither know nor care that you forgave or didn't forgive them as they are blissfully getting on with their lives totally oblivious to the effect they are having on yours. They have left you bringing the past into the present and making it into your future. Is that what you want for yourself?

What about trying something different? Would you be willing to accept that sometimes things happen in our lives that we have no control over apart from how we react to the situation? Acceptance does not mean forgiveness. It means coming to terms with what happened and moving on. Nobody said you had to like it but surely it has to be better than this festering hatred you are inflicting on yourself. Notice that I said you are inflicting this upon yourself. No one else is doing this to you. Someone else might have created the event but now you are letting them hurt you over and over on a daily basis and to what end. It serves no purpose other than keeping you stuck in a past of bitterness and self-recrimination. What have you got to lose by letting go of this pain?

You have a choice to make. You can either hold on to the grudge in the vain hope that something useful will actually come from it and then it will magically disappear, or you can decide to accept that it is something that happened and now it's time to let it go. Imagine what it would be like never having to think about it again. You don't have to imagine; you have to decide. Hopefully, you will make the right decision. When you hold a grudge, you effectively hand control of your life over to the person that caused it. Surely you don't want someone to have that sort of power over you?

Why do some people fake depression? Is it for attention?

This question is considerably more complex than it first appears. There are unquestionably some people that fake depression for attention. We live in an age where social media is king and the number of likes someone receives can come to define the value of that person. It seems that if you are popular, even for being depressed, then you are a somebody. If you aren't popular, it can feel like you are a nobody. I find this a terribly sad reflection of the society we live in today.

Just so we are clear when someone fakes depression they are not actually faking the mental illness they are faking what they *think* depression is. I don't think it is possible to fake serious depression unless you have experienced it firsthand. The internet is awash with information about depression the same way it is awash with information on how to drive a car. I am sure you would agree reading about driving a car is not really the same as driving one. The same applies to having depression.

However, there is a darker side to the whole faking depression phenomenon that is going around at the moment. What if the person is *actually* depressed but can't find it within themselves to talk to someone? Isn't it sad they only feel safe sharing their pain with anonymous strangers on the internet? Depression can be a life-changing illness, even faking depression can lead to full-blown depression itself especially if the person is already feeling vulnerable and feel they have no one to turn to.

Human beings perform behaviors for a reason; they do not exist in isolation. If someone feels the need to fake depression there's a reason behind it. Would it not be better to find out the reasons behind such behavior rather than brushing it aside as crying out for attention. What if it's a cry for help we are ignoring? The person might not even be aware of the reason themselves, but a reason still exists. Humans are very complex. To an outsider, these actions don't make any sense because it's not something we would do ourselves. However, we are not them, we don't have their needs and wants.

Celebrity culture. You cannot have helped but notice the trend of celebs *coming out* and detailing their struggles with depression and anxiety. Why this is happening is anyone's guess. Maybe they are the grown-up version of the teen on the internet looking for likes. We certainly know they like the attention. Not all celebs are doing it for this reason of course. Some of them have a genuine desire to help destigmatize a serious mental health issue. Unfortunately, by a strange quirk, those same celebs have unwittingly made depression a cool thing to have. Those same teens we talked about earlier are following their virtual heroes online and attempting to emulate their very real illnesses in an attempt to look cool themselves. The younger the celeb the better. Never underestimate the desire to be seen as one cool kid even if the price of admission is belonging to a club where everybody seemingly has mental health issues.

Can making mistakes cause depression?

Making mistakes won't cause depression but obsessing about those mistakes certainly can. All too often we can make a simple mistake into something wrong with us. We can easily view it as some sort of character flaw that makes us a failure. If we start obsessing about this it can easily step over the line into self-recrimination, criticizing ourselves, seeing ourselves as not being good enough and being judgmental about ourselves. When that happens all the ingredients are in place to open the door to an episode of depression. Let's see if we can stop it in its tracks, shall we?

Ask yourself this question: "Have you learned anything in this life without making a mistake first?" Do you remember the first time you tried to drive a car? Did you just jump in the driving seat, and everything was perfect from day one? If you did then there is no need to read any further as you are perfect. That's the problem; we want to achieve the unachievable, we want everything to work out perfectly and have no errors. The only problem with that is we don't live in a perfect world. The human condition means we can only learn by our mistakes. From learning to walk to driving a car and everything in between we only learned by making mistakes and moving on from them.

Let's examine what you are doing when you beat yourself up for a mistake and then you can decide if it makes any sense. You are here in the present, and with the benefit of hindsight you are looking into the past and beating yourself up because you made a decision based on the available knowledge you had to hand at that time.

If you had a time machine and went back to the past armed with only the knowledge you had then, you would make the same mistake again. You didn't have the knowledge then that you have now. You didn't have a crystal ball that was able to predict whether your decision was going to be the correct one in the future. So what do you think? Does it seem like a good idea now to punish yourself harshly for past mistakes? If your answer is still yes, then ask yourself what the punishment will achieve. It won't stop you from making mistakes in the future. Making mistakes is just an integral part of the human experience. If we can learn from them, so much the better. If we don't then that is a mistake.

There will be people reading this, and maybe you are one of those people that will be thinking "if I treat myself harshly for my mistakes it will prevent me from making the same mistake again." Ask yourself this question: "When in your life has negative motivation ever worked for you?" When you were a child and were proud of some achievement only for someone to make fun of it or worse still berate you for it and tell you that you could have done better, how did that feel? Did it make you feel good about yourself, or did it make you feel small and unworthy? This is exactly what you are doing to yourself when you try and use negative motivation as a method to push you to bigger and better things. It didn't work then, and it won't work now.

One last thing for you to think about. Instead of asking yourself *how* to stop beating yourself up over your mistakes ask yourself *why* you are beating yourself up and what does it achieve? Take back your power, acknowledge your mistake, and move on.

How come I miss the feeling of being depressed?

I know what you are thinking, "how in the hell could anyone miss the feeling of being depressed?" But, with depression, things are rarely that straightforward. I completely understand why someone that has never suffered the illness would find this a hard concept to swallow. Believe it or not, it's not all that unusual as I will explain. For ease of explanation, I am going to use the example of someone called Dave.

Dave had suffered reactive depression for almost five years. Then, with a combination of medication and therapy, he started to recover and thought that was the end of it. However, within a year he reported that he started to miss the feeling depression gave him but couldn't understand why. Naturally, he was confused, who wouldn't be? What he didn't realize was this was a process he was going through.

First, he was depressed and then his mind adapted to the depression through a process called hedonic adaptation. There is nothing the mind likes more than patterns of behavior and consistency. These dysfunctional patterns become very familiar to the depressed mind. At an unconscious level, it can feel like the sort of craving a smoker might experience. As far as the mind is concerned it wants you to repeat these patterns to fulfill a need in the psyche. It doesn't much care if these behaviors are bad for you; it just craves the familiarity of consistency.

Next, Dave, with the help of some professional intervention was on the road to recovery but reported that sometimes in the background he felt like something was missing. What Dave was missing was the familiarity his mind has become accustomed to.

Think of it this way. When someone suffers depression, they lay down neural pathways the same way a skater lays down grooves on ice. The neural pathways of depression might be deactivated with professional help, but they can still exist as a memory. A bit like when the skater leaves the ice, the grooves don't disappear just because they are not getting used.

Dave's mind craved the familiarity and consistency it had become used to. When someone suffers from depression for an extended period of time it can leave a mark on the psyche that can be quite difficult to erase even with the passage of time—such is the complexity of the illness and also the reason why relapses are quite common. Is this something you should be worried about? Not really, but it is something you should be aware of. On the face of it, this can seem quite trivial and not important enough to report to your therapist. I would have to disagree as it has the *potential* to develop into a relapse. It's much better to nip it in the bud, so to speak. If it's important to you it should be important to whoever is looking after you. Do not be afraid to speak up as depression likes nothing more than being ignored so that it can get deeper and harder to treat in the background.

Needless to say, not everyone is going to experience this phenomenon as everybody experiences depression completely differently; no two people are the same. It's just something I thought might be a good idea to bring to your attention. Forewarned is forearmed, so they say. If in doubt, talk it out.

How to respond to a depressed friend when they say "I'm fine"

No matter how counter-intuitive it might seem, if the person says they are *fine* it's a clear indication to you to back off because they are dealing with something, and they do not want your input or help. You have to remember that the illness of depression can cause someone to think very irrationally at times. They can push away the very thing that could help them. They can say they are fine when in actual fact they are anything but. They shut down when actually opening up would probably help them.

If you really feel the need to say something further you could go with "I just asked because you are looking a bit down, if you need my help or want to talk, just ask."

This is supportive and non-intrusive, which is exactly what your depressed friend wants. Always be guided with what *they* want not what *you* think they should want because that becomes about *your* needs instead of theirs. I absolutely get it that you want to help. Just make sure you have their permission and they have asked you for it. Don't assume you know them better than they know themselves. Try and understand that at times communication and interaction with other people can be excruciatingly difficult for a depressed person.

They are trying to protect themselves from feeling like a burden. At times it's much easier to pretend that everything is fine than it is to tell you how they are actually feeling because that would mean having to drop the socially acceptable mask they feel the need to wear to let you in. Does all this sound confusing? Welcome to the world of a depressed person where confusion and frustration reign supreme.

Of course, there is another scenario you should consider. When they say they are fine it might be because at the moment they actually are. Don't ruin it by asking "are you sure?" because now you have very subtly accused them of lying to you. You are also very covertly telling them that you know them better than they know themselves and their emotions. Whether you meant it that way or not is immaterial because potentially that's how it is going to come across.

One last thing to consider. Most depressed people that I have met are holding back a tsunami of emotion. They live in constant fear that if they start talking about their depression, they won't be able to stop, with all the stigma, prejudice, discrimination and potential social isolation that could entail. They also live in fear that their revelation could be met with "yeah, life's tough" or something similar. The last thing they want is to be met with platitude as this only serves to trivialize their very real suffering.

Always be guided by what the depressed person wants. If they want to talk, great. If they don't want to talk, great. Just remind them you are there if they need you. Unless you follow these few simple rules, you will very quickly find yourself on the outside looking in as the depressed person will find a way to isolate you, so they don't have to feel under pressure. Nobody said dealing with depression was easy. Good luck!

Why do I keep reliving past negative experiences? It's depressing.

There is absolutely nothing your mind likes more than patterns and consistency. Reliving past negative experiences is a pattern that eventually forms into a habit which in turn turns into a self-perpetuating loop of negativity. In other words, the more you do it the more familiar it becomes and the more the mind gives you more of the same.

I am going to give you a suggestion and depending on your state of mind and your willingness to do the work you will either think it's a great idea or you will file it under *maybe later* and never return to it. Will it work for everyone for every type of problem? There's nothing in this whole book that works for everyone one hundred percent of the time. It's something for you to try that might enable you to break the pattern you currently find yourself in. It might help if you find yourself a pen and some paper for this exercise. Writing stuff down can be very cathartic.

Take those past negative experiences one at a time and find the lesson they taught you because they are there if you are willing to look for them. Note I didn't say put a positive gloss on those events because all that is doing is resisting reality. I also didn't say use it as an excuse to beat yourself up either. You have to separate yourself from the emotion and look at these events clinically. Emotion only gets in the way of rational thought. Make a real effort to stay away from how these events made you feel as that will keep you stuck in the emotion.

Can you drill down into each of these events and find something you can use in the present? Did some event teach you to be more careful in the future . . . you get the idea? Maybe it was a mistake you made; can it teach you not to make the same mistake again? Did you make a decision that in hindsight wasn't the correct one? How could you possibly have known at that time it was a bad decision, you couldn't see into the future? This is how analytical you need to be. If you find yourself getting agitated or angry it's a sure sign you have drifted back into the emotions and you need to start over.

At the minute you are on a hamster wheel revisiting the past and hoping this time will be different, that maybe something will have changed to make you feel better about it. That won't happen because of our inbuilt bias toward negativity. If anything it will make you feel worse as you are reinforcing the negative memory every time you access it. Separating yourself from the emotion will allow you to look at the issue dispassionately. You are the one in control here. Emotions don't attack us, we create them.

Maybe it's time you got off the wheel and took a step back so that you can look objectively at your past and make something useful out of it that you can use in the present. Will it change the past? Definitely not. What it might do however is allow you to think differently about the past and move on from the vicious circle you find yourself caught up in. The past is a great place to visit but I wouldn't want to live there. Accepting that sometimes bad things happen over which we have no control is your first step hopefully to emotional freedom. I hope you give my suggestion a try.

I'm too nice. I always care about people and try not to hurt them. I have a weak personality and always have depression. People always use and manipulate me. I'm tired. How do I change?

I am including this question in the hope someone reading this might find it resonates with them. This is a question that was asked of me on an internet forum along with the complete answer I gave them. I think it illustrates nicely how a faulty belief can lead to all sorts of complications and when left unchallenged like in this case can lead to feelings of inadequacy and possibly depression.

Everything you have described above has a belief system propping up the whole house of cards. It's something you might not even be aware of until I say it. From my remote perspective, you have an *"I'm not good enough"* belief about yourself. That belief is the glue that holds everything together and keeps everything that you have described in place. Let's unpack it bit by bit.

I'm too nice. I always care about people and try not to hurt them.

There's nothing wrong with being nice until it very quietly slips into people pleasing. We do this in an attempt to make people like us because we really don't like ourselves very much. In an attempt not to hurt them we end up hurting ourselves. If we keep giving bits of ourselves away, we end up with nothing of ourselves.

I have a weak personality and always have depression.

No, you just don't have any boundaries. When we let people constantly cross our boundaries, we turn that resentment inwards and it is expressed as depression/anxiety. We are teaching people every day of the week how they should treat us. Think of it this way, if you are getting treated like a doormat you first had to lie on the floor.

People always use and manipulate me. I'm tired.

No, people don't use and manipulate you; you have inadvertently *allowed* the using and manipulation to occur. To change other people's behavior toward you, you have to change the behavior toward yourself. Ask yourself *why* you have allowed other people to manipulate you? Do you feel they are superior to you?

How do I change?

Commit to stopping people pleasing starting today because it will never work as a long-term strategy. People pleasers get used and manipulated, not liked . . . sound familiar? Commit to establishing boundaries and enforcing them daily. If people don't respect our boundaries, we give off the message we have no respect for ourselves. When we don't feel we are respected it is expressed as feelings of depression; we feel we have no autonomy. Changing a core belief can take time. If you want to accelerate the process and make sure you are on track, an appointment with a therapist might prove useful.

I'm too nice (update)

This person got in contact with me a few months after giving them this answer and told me they did indeed contact a therapist and they discovered this faulty belief went right back to their childhood. Apparently, the parents played their siblings off against each other and rewarded the more successful of the two while admonishing the other.

The parents used love as a stick to beat them with. In other words, the siblings had to compete for parental attention. Is it any wonder one or both of them felt they weren't good enough because in essence, that's exactly what they were being told? The original poster of the question turned to people pleasing as a way of garnering the love from other people that he never got from his parents. He was looking externally for something he didn't have for himself; love.

This is not as uncommon as you might think. We all have different methods of navigating our lives. Some people lie, some people manipulate, and some people use their sexuality to bend people to their way of thinking. Advertising is doing it to you every day of the week. Did you really buy that new car because you *actually* needed it, or did you buy it because of the way it made you feel? I digress.

I am happy to report this person stopped the people pleasing and set himself good boundaries that were reinforced on a daily basis. He no longer needs the validation of others to give him value as he always had value, he just didn't realize it. This is why I always recommend professional help because it's impossible to change something that is hidden. A good therapist will guide you to bring that which is hidden out into the open and hopefully help you find a resolution.

What are some subtle things that can erode our mental health over time and can potentially nudge the door open to depression?

- Constantly comparing ourselves to other people. If we do this, we normally place ourselves at the bottom of the heap. It's not easy to feel good about yourself when you feel you are looking up from the gutter.

- Obsessing about what others think of us. Truth is, unless we *directly* affect them, they scarcely recognize our existence. We are thinking about them, they are mostly not thinking about us.

- Telling ourselves we are *not good enough*. This is like a constant drip-feed of acid to our self-esteem.

- Extreme people pleasing. We all like to be liked. When that turns into a *need* to be liked where other people's needs are more important than yours, then you have a problem.

- Pain. Constant pain can lead to a downward spiral of depression and feeling trapped. We can feel we have lost personal autonomy if we don't have control over our own bodies.

- Lack of confidence. Lack of confidence can make us feel very isolated and insular. It can make us feel the whole world is confident, except us. Social media tends to amplify those feelings.

- Family disputes. It's difficult to accept that the very people that *should* love and care for you, don't.

- Bullying. Bullying at any age can have devastating effects that can last well into adulthood and possibly a lifetime; it strikes at our very core.

- Disturbed or lack of sleep over the long term. The link between depression and sleep problems has been well established.

- Caring for someone with mental health issues. It's very common for the carer to be affected by the deterioration of another's mental health especially if they are in a close relationship.

- Undermining. Passive-aggressive behaviors and getting constantly undermined will affect mental health in the long term. This is especially so in a marriage where the victim feels they cannot escape this abuse.

- Perfectionism. Perfectionism goes hand in hand with never feeling that what you do is ever good enough. Chasing the elusive dream of perfection serves to intensify those feelings.

- Loneliness and isolation. Isolation is a major symptom of depression. We tend to isolate ourselves from the very people that can help us; such is the complexity of this distressing illness.

- Having someone negative in our lives that we cannot avoid; it's like constantly rubbing salt into an open wound.

- Not being recognized as an individual in a relationship. We are not extensions of other people. Personal autonomy is vital for mental health. We are not just cooks, cleaners, general dogsbody and someone to have sex with occasionally.

- Culture. Yes, culture. This is where the person can be reduced to nothing more than a possession that is subjugated and restricted at every opportunity with threats of abuse, or worse.

- Non-acceptance. If we consistently deny that our life has changed and things will never be the same, it can become a fast track to depression.

- Living in the past and pining for how things used to be. It's extremely difficult to move forward if we are constantly looking over our shoulder to where we came from.

- Expectation. If our expectations of other people don't match reality, we are going to have a hard time. We are projecting what *we* would like them to be, not how they actually are.

- Trying to change the behavior of another person when they see no compelling reason to change is a one-way ticket to frustration and disappointment.

There are loads of other factors that can lead to a slow deterioration of mental health, but I would rather not keep you reading for the next week. The good thing about most of the above is they can be overcome with self-regulation, those that can't fall into the domain of professional help.

How do I motivate my depressed mind?

It's very true that one of the first things to fly out of the window when someone suffers depression is motivation. The illness seems to drain them of the very thing that could help them. Self-motivation under normal circumstances is difficult. Self-motivation when depressed is nearly impossible. Maybe if we look at the way some people find motivation, we could adapt it to motivating someone through depression.

People that are motivated seem to be so by the application of external influences. Let me ask you a question. Which was the most successful in your quest to lose some weight? Was it when you kept it to yourself or was it when you told people you were going to lose some weight and combined that with going to the gym or some other activity where you could be seen? I think most people would have probably said the latter. Why is that? It's because we are inclined to be more motivated when we are held accountable. Also, our environment can play a huge part in our efforts.

I will ask another similar question. Did you work harder when you joined a gym or work harder when you exercised at home? Again, I think most people would say the latter because not only is the atmosphere in a gym conducive to working harder they have also committed financial resources to their quest. What has all this got to do with depression you may ask?

If we are motivated by external influences what would happen do you think if we managed to rope someone into making us accountable for doing ten minutes of walking per day for instance? Or catching up with someone you haven't spoken to in a while because you have been isolating yourself away from the world.

This might not sound like much but believe me, I know from personal experience it can have a profound effect on your levels of motivation over a period of time. How could you integrate this into your life? Could you partake in a variation of my idea and find a way to make yourself accountable to someone else? What about joining a support group in your area?

There's a reason top athletes have coaches and trainers. The truth is the athlete probably knows more than the coach and the trainer combined about whatever sport they are engaged in. They both hold the athlete accountable which in turn motivates the athlete to do better. They can also point out some blind spots the athlete is not aware of, but their main job is the application of the mental game. Like I said previously, your environment plays a huge part in motivation. You don't need me to tell you that staring at four walls with only misery for company isn't very inspiring. To get your motivation moving you need to remove yourself from this environment, even if it is only for twenty minutes per day. Over a period of time, you will notice the difference. At the moment your mind has become accustomed to the routine you engage in. If you engage in a new routine like I have suggested, eventually it will become the new norm with all the beneficial effects that flow from it. Will it be easy? No, it will probably be the hardest thing you have done in your life but also the most rewarding.

How do I help a friend that refuses professional help for their depression?

That is certainly a tough one because how exactly do you get someone to accept help when they don't want it? The first thing you need to realize is that your depressed friend has to take the first step. They have to *want* to get better and be willing to be proactive to make it a reality. Nothing is going to change that simple truth.

You could ask them directly what they are afraid of that is preventing them from reaching out for help. Maybe they are scared of going to a therapist on their own in which case it might be possible for you to accompany them to a session or two. Fear of the unknown can be a powerful barrier to taking the first step. Learned helplessness is a very real thing I have covered in another chapter. If they don't want to visit a therapist face-to-face in an office setting, would they be willing to do it virtually? Since COVID-19 an awful lot of therapists have moved their services online. The world is literally their oyster.

The secret is to find out what is preventing them from wanting to move forward and try to gently address those issues with them in a kind and compassionate manner. On no account try and use tough love in an effort to get them to move. Resorting to either guilt or shame will prove absolutely ineffective and will more than likely result in you losing a friend. Your friend is already feeling bad enough without an extra layer of guilt for them to cope with. Negative criticism never works. Not now, not ever. Always think of your role in this relationship as one of support and understanding. Take the lead from your depressed friend and know when to back off as this is going to be a difficult time for you both. This is about what *they* want, not what you want.

Does the person want to talk about their depression, great? Does the person not want to talk about their depression, great? You have to be able to go with the flow and adapt to the situation as it unfolds. You absolutely have got to let the depressed person take the lead. There is no harm at all in making suggestions, just know when to back off when it is obvious the suggestions are not being well received.

There will be a lot of holding your tongue involved when you are trying to help a depressed person, but it gets easier with practice. Just remember the depressed person might not want to get help at the moment, but that could all change next week—be patient and definitely do not try and force the issue. Depression has a nasty habit of sucking willpower and motivation from a person. Unfortunately, these are the very things they will need to enable them to reach out for help and it is something you cannot give them.

It might not be very politically correct to say it but trying to help someone through depression can be very hard work. There will be plenty of times you will feel like walking away which is exactly what all my friends did as I went through ten years of depression. Looking back on it now, I can't honestly say I blame them. So what are some practical suggestions for helping someone?

Be a great listener. Sometimes the depressed person just needs to let off some steam, so to speak. They are not expecting you to *fix* them. They already know this is going to be a hard journey that will have to be taken alone. Believe me, a friendly ear goes a long way.

Can you do some practical things for them? Would you be willing to go out and do some grocery shopping for them? What about taking care of some of their bills online for them? Depression is exhausting, and anything you can do to ease the burden will be appreciated.

Lastly, look after yourself. Create boundaries and stick to them. You are there to support them; you are not their therapist. You can't always help someone who won't help themselves, but you can show them you care.

Lastly, I would like you to pay close attention to your own mental health in this scenario. It is extremely easy to fall into the trap of rescuer and fixer which you are neither. Doing so can have a detrimental effect on *you* and place *you* on a slippery slope to problems of your own. Don't jump into the mire with them or you will both end up going under. Your role is to throw a rope if needed. Their role is to grab the rope and accept the help.

I wish you well and thank you for being there for your friend.

Should I tell other people about my depression?

In an ideal world telling other people that you are suffering from depression would be a great idea as it could potentially help with the feelings of isolation and loneliness commonly associated with depression. Unfortunately, we don't live in an ideal world, prejudice; stigma and discrimination are very much alive and kicking and can come from some very unexpected sources.

I have personally been told by a psychiatrist that I should "trust more in the Lord" and this would be my pathway to a cure. I wonder did he ever stop to think about the effect this would have on me? Now, not only am I suffering depression, I am also being punished by God for my lack of faith—hardly a recipe for success, is it?

Nothing would please me more than to give you a definitive answer to the vexed question of telling other people about your mental health issues. Unfortunately, no *one-size-fits-all* answer exists. It can only ever be a personal choice based on your environment, how much you trust the person and even your culture. The experience of someone suffering depression in India is hugely different from someone in America. Culture can play a big role in your decision and that decision should not be taken lightly.

Trust is another big factor to consider. Can you trust the person you are telling to not spread your revelation further than you would like? Can you trust them to not use this information against you sometime in the future? If you can answer *yes* to both those questions then by all means, confide in this person, it will certainly benefit you enormously.

Unfortunately, we have not evolved to the point that we can talk about mental health as easily as we talk about something we have seen on television the night before. I wish the opposite were true and hopefully, in the future, it will be. Until then you might have to grow a bit of a thick skin to counter some of the unexpected reactions you might experience.

People by their nature retreat to well-established patterns of behavior such as denial or dismissal when they are confronted with something they feel uncomfortable about. Try not to take it personally if someone says "Don't worry you will get over it" or "What have you got to be depressed about?" This is an extremely common experience for people suffering depression and is merely a projection of the other person's insecurities.

I wish you well if you decide to share your *news* with other people and I sincerely hope you find someone to confide in; it really can make all the difference, just choose very carefully.

Do some people enjoy their depression?

I know this might seem like an alien concept especially to someone that has endured the horrors of depression. After all, how could someone *enjoy* suffering? I think we need to change the narrative slightly to understand what is going on here. Before we start, I should add that the number of people I am referring to is minuscule, but this phenomenon does exist especially among the younger generation.

I don't think these people actually *enjoy* feelings of hopelessness, helplessness and powerlessness. However, I do think some people enjoy the *perceived benefits* of being known as having depression. Human behavior does not exist in a vacuum, in other words, we do everything for a reason, there is a perceived payoff. It ticks a psychological box, so to speak.

The perceived payoff could be the attention someone receives from other people especially on social media where someone thinks their worth is determined by how many *likes* they get. It is quite common to see pictures of young people *being depressed* when actually they have no concept of the devastation depression can bring into someone's life. Naturally, there will be some people that do suffer depression. They are very much in the minority.

Another powerful motivator is sympathy. Some people enjoy the sympathy they get from friends, family and the occasional therapist that is not doing their job correctly because they became entangled in the story of their client. Sympathy can also include special treatment by others. Friends and family walk on eggshells and are very careful what they say and do around the sufferer as they don't want to be responsible for sending the person into a deeper depressive state with all the consequences that entail. For some, it can be a form of control in a life that seems out of control.

Lastly, for some people there can be a financial benefit to their illness. The Government has officially sanctioned them as unfit to work, a powerful validation indeed, and gives them a monthly payment to aid their recovery. Unfortunately, this can have the complete opposite effect and take away the motivation to get better.

I understand this chapter can seem a little bit controversial and make for uncomfortable reading. My intention was not to offend it but to illustrate that human behavior is very seldom black and white; there are hundreds of shades of nuance. I make no judgment as to why someone does what they do. Hopefully, you won't either and come away with a better understanding of what can drive some people.

Why can't I figure out and conquer my depression?

Depression has the ability to rob a person of the very tools that could help them recover. Let me start with an analogy of what I mean to help get some perspective. Imagine you are a lightweight boxer and you have been drawn to fight against the heavyweight champion of the world. It would be safe to assume you are going to get knocked to the ground, a lot. Eventually, you are not going to get up only to be knocked down again.

Depression can be a bit like that; it can make someone feel helpless in the face of insurmountable odds. One of the first things that fly out the window when depression comes knocking at the door is motivation. It is excruciatingly difficult to motivate yourself when every atom of your body is screaming to just give up and give in. Even the simplest tasks like brushing your teeth or showering can become a monumental task.

When someone is this depressed the most common thing to go through their mind is "what's the point?" Unfortunately, they don't realize this mindset is feeding their depression and keeping them stuck in a loop of misery. Severe depression has the ability to shut someone down so completely it is not uncommon to hear of people that literally can't function for weeks at a time.

Another tool depression can rob a person of is the energy to fight it. What most people that have never experienced depression don't realize is how exhausting it is to battle with this illness on a daily basis. It takes up so much real estate in the mind it seems to exclude everything else, it is front and center of a person's thoughts for most if not all of the day. That combined with disrupted sleep which is very common in depression, and you have all the ingredients in place for the perfect storm. Lack of energy and motivation are the terrible twins that turn up at your door uninvited and then refuse to leave.

How exactly does someone with severe depression motivate themselves to exercise when they have neither the will nor the energy to get out of bed? In the case of severe depression if by some miracle they managed to motivate themselves and had enough energy to exercise and then failed, this, in turn, would lead to a cascade of self-recrimination and even self-loathing which in turn feeds the illness. With depression, a one-size-fits-all approach never works. Sometimes it can feel like *damned if you do, damned if you don't*—such is the complexity of this mental health issue.

There will of course be people reading this chapter that will not recognize themselves in any of the above as it doesn't apply to them. To those people, I would say count yourself very lucky that you still have the motivation and the energy to continue the fight. For some people, the fight has been knocked out of them just like the boxer from before and they have drifted into learned helplessness. Professional intervention is normally required at this point. This is what life can be like at the severe end of the scale of depression.

How can I make myself immune from depression?

Unfortunately, asking this question is somewhat akin to asking, "How can I make myself immune from thinking?" Because in its most basic form that is what depression is, a reaction to one's own thinking. Obviously, there is a lot more to depression than that, but you get the idea. Let me put it another way. If we could flick a switch inside our head that turned off the ability to think we wouldn't suffer depression.

I have to admit to a wry smile when I hear someone answering this question by saying "get regular exercise," "eat fresh green vegetables" or my personal favorite "listen to music." Certainly, these things can *help* alleviate depression to a degree, but make someone *immune* to it . . . I don't think so. If these suggestions made any sense, it would mean anyone that goes to a gym, or is religious, a vegetarian or a musician has an automatic immunity from depression. That is so patently not true it would be slightly laughable if it wasn't so serious.

As I have said before elsewhere in this book, depression is equal opportunities. It doesn't much care who you are or what you do, if it's your turn, it's your turn. I so wish the opposite was true, unfortunately, that isn't living in reality. Like I said earlier, some of these things can help alleviate depression, by no stretch of the imagination do they give someone a free pass. Now that we have established that there is no such thing as immunity to depression what can you do to help yourself through an episode?

Please note what follows is not a cure for depression, it's just some hints to help you through a rocky patch. Naturally, the effects will be varied depending on the type and severity of the illness.

Getting proper sleep. Resist the urge to sleep during the day as this can quickly develop into a particularly nasty habit that makes things worse in the long term. Also, sleeping outside normal bedtimes can have a seriously detrimental effect on the body clock with all the ramifications that come with it.

Stay off social media. Let's face it, social media is overflowing with people pretending to be someone they aren't. The downside of this is we compare our lives to these carefully constructed illusions and then engage in criticizing ourselves for not being the same. This is the last thing you need to be doing at this time.

Stay off alcohol. It's a depressant, hardly the thing you want to be putting into your system when you are already depressed.

Exercise. If you can physically bring yourself to do it, I would recommend some form of gentle exercise; the effects of the feel-good chemicals on the brain are well documented.

Reach out. This can be especially difficult when every atom of your existence is telling you to isolate yourself away from other people. I would encourage you to try even if you have to force yourself. There are other methods; these are some of the easier ones.

How do I know if I am depressed or just lazy?

Imagine this.

You are sitting on your couch looking out the window when suddenly a gust of wind blows a piece of paper onto the glass and you realize it's a $50 bill. You get off the couch, scratch your butt and go outside and retrieve the money. On the way back you go to the fridge and get yourself another beer and then return to the ass-shaped hollow on your couch.

Now the same scenario with someone suffering depression.

You see the $50 bill stuck to the glass and you think to yourself "I really should go out and get that." Unfortunately, those thoughts will quickly be replaced with "why bother, what would I spend it on anyhow?" "I'm too tired. Maybe someone will come along and bring it inside to me."

There's another gust of wind and the $50 bill takes off never to be seen again.

That's when the self-flagellation start . . .

- I *should* have gone outside and got it.

- What kind of *useless* human being am I anyhow?

- I *should* have stayed in bed.

- I have *no* luck.

This beating could probably go on for the next few hours or so as they stare at the spot where the money used to be wondering where life went so wrong.

That's the difference.

I hope you understand all of the above was a bit tongue in cheek and used only to illustrate the helplessness that comes with chronic depression. It's not that the person doesn't want to go and get the $50 bill, it's because they have lost the ability and the motivation. If it doesn't help their depression, they see no reason to take any action.

Chronic depression can make someone feel dead and lifeless. As someone I know once put it: "It's like wearing a lead coat that you are never allowed to take off." I think that's a very apt description, the feeling of heaviness a person experiences can be overpowering and all-consuming. If the depression is really severe a person can get to a point that they don't even care if they get better and suicide seems a better option than suffering the torment day in day out.

Searching for happiness (Part 1)

What good would a book about depression be if it didn't contain at least one chapter about happiness to balance it out? I have a small confession to make. I lifted this chapter from one of my other books because I think it is so relevant. Hopefully, this chapter will give you food for thought and a different perspective on happiness.

At first glance, searching for happiness seems a worthwhile endeavor, doesn't it? Yes, providing we're looking in the right places. Why can we search for happiness for a lifetime and never find it? Is it because we're too *unhappy* to find it. Could it be we don't deserve to be happy and are doomed to a life of misery?

Maybe we don't have enough money; we're not attractive enough, intelligent enough or plain not good enough. It's none of those things; we haven't found happiness because we're looking in the wrong places. Happiness can't and never will be found in anything external to you. Read that statement again. It's of vital importance you grasp what it means, no matter how counter-intuitive it seems.

When you think of the word 'happiness,' what does it look like to you? Does it look like a new car, new house, new job, new husband, wife or partner? Maybe it looks like $1,000,000 in your bank account. It might look like all of the above and beyond. Unfortunately, none of these things are going to make you happy. They can certainly stimulate you and produce a feeling we have come to know as happiness. But real lasting happiness . . .?

Here's the thing—we still continue to believe those desires external to us produce happiness. That's why we spend a lifetime chasing them. When we acquire those desires, it makes us feel good. They stimulate the brain to release feel-good chemicals into our system, and this *feeling* is what we've come to associate with happiness. So the search continues, and we try and repeat the process over and over again, always chasing our next hit of dopamine. We are chasing our own tail in the hope of catching it. We appear to be stuck on the roller coaster of intermittent highs, followed by the inevitable lows. It reminds me of a story I once read. You've probably heard a version of it before, but in case you haven't here it is.

A man loses his keys in the front garden of his house; he phones his friend and asks her to help him find them. The woman turns up, only to find the man looking for his keys under a streetlight opposite his house. Naturally, she asks him why he's looking for his keys over there when he said he lost them in the garden. The man replies, "Because it's brighter over here."

Happiness can be thought about in a similar fashion. We're attracted to the bright things in the mistaken belief that novelty will bring us happiness. We're bombarded by messages every minute of every day via advertising which tells us happiness can be found in wearing a certain perfume, buying a certain car, losing weight, looking more attractive, getting a big house and a big job, and a million other ways that will stimulate our insecurity. They don't mention the debt, of course.

How many people, yourself included, have found true happiness in the possession of any of these things?

No one has ever found a lifetime of happiness in something external to themselves. Stimulation, yes. Novelty, yes. Happiness, no. Hedonic adaptation is at play in your search for the thing you think will make your life complete. You adapt over a period of time to anything positive or negative in your life, and there are no grey areas here. It's simply how your brain works. It's what helped us evolve.

As a species, we're insatiable; never happy with what we have. Thousands of years ago this insatiability served a purpose but combine that with hedonic adaptation and we have the perfect storm for promoting unhappiness. On the one hand, we have insatiability driving us to achieve and possess, while on the other hand, we have adaptation. So we're driven to obtain, then we adapt to what we've obtained, ensuring the cycle is repeated again and again.

For the most part, this happens at a subconscious level. The one thing we do know, however, is that at a conscious level, we aren't happy. No matter how hard we try, happiness seems out of reach or fleeting at best. Something other people seem to have, but not us. Except what you observe isn't always what it seems.

You are contrasting what you are seeing through a filter of how you feel about yourself. If you feel unhappy, you seem to be surrounded by happy people. You've made an assumption based on zero evidence. As humans, we only see what we want to see, not reality. And that seeing is tainted by emotion and feelings. Those other people are searching for happiness as well. Just because we can't see it, doesn't mean it's not happening.

As a species, we lie to each other about our levels of happiness. When asked how we are, we reply, "Fine" even if we're dying inside. We would rather eat a wasp than tell the truth. Such is the delusion of happiness. The stark reality is if we're all so happy, why does every survey report that despite us never having had it so good, we've never been more miserable and unhappy? Especially so in developed countries.

Take for example someone who wins the lottery. Most people would assume they would be the happiest people on the planet after winning so much money. Most lottery winners return to the same level of happiness/unhappiness they had within one year of their big win. It makes sense, as we now know adaptation and homeostasis are at play here. Don't take my word for it, look it up for yourself. It makes for some pretty interesting reading. If you decide to stop chasing happiness, what then?

You could pursue peace of mind as a viable alternative. What's peace of mind? It's what you will be left with once you drop the nonsense of expectation, complaining, judging, worry, guilt and everything else you've been reading about. Remove those obstacles and you'll reach the core of who you really are. The real you, the one who craves a peaceful mind, unencumbered with the baggage everyone else has to suffer.

But, to get there it is necessary to know why the pursuit of the thing you call 'happiness' is holding you back.

Searching for happiness (Part 2)

Happiness is a word loaded with expectation, isn't it? We think we should be happy, but we also think we shouldn't have to work to achieve it. Somehow, we have a misguided belief that happiness should be our default position. Actually, no, survival is our default position, and this survival mechanism doesn't really care much whether you're happy or not. Your brain uses twenty percent of the energy you consume in a day. It hasn't a clue what happiness is.

As far as your brain is concerned, happiness doesn't exist. Happiness is only a label given to a feeling which at best could be thought of as stimulation through novelty. So let's take a look at the areas of our life where we chase the carrot of happiness, only to find the stick of disappointment.

Relationships. How selfish must we be to imagine another person should make us happy? It's never said aloud, of course, but if we rely on finding happiness through another person, the expectation is there. Sometimes the other person plays our game of expectation, especially in the early days of a relationship. Then the rot sets in.

Remember, happiness, as defined earlier, requires the other person to be a source of continual stimulation and excitement, and this is required to last indefinitely.

Worse still, in an attempt to rekindle the closeness of the early days of the relationship, our couple decides to have a child, only to find the addition of another person, and the responsibility it entails drives them further apart.

Happiness can't be found in another person unless the other person is willing to suppress their personality completely to fit your worldview.

If our couple manages to survive the upheaval, a maturity enters the relationship and also a deeper understanding of how it should proceed. Each partner is independent of the other but staying in the relationship out of choice. This happens, for the most part, at a subconscious level. It isn't written down anywhere, nor a contract signed.

Consider bringing this level of maturity to *any* relationship you have. Remove the expectation you have of the other person to make you happy or fulfilled as they really don't deserve that kind of pressure. Allow the other person to be *completely* independent of your needs and wants. It takes a great deal of emotional maturity and honesty to look at your relationships. It also takes a great deal of introspection and awareness to admit you might be doing what I've described.

Are you in a relationship where you *expect* the other person to make you happy and complete you? There's only one way to find out, and that's by doing the hard work of self-introspection and awareness. Most people don't.

Validation and approval. On the face of it, seeking validation and approval for your actions seems pretty harmless, doesn't it? Well, it is if we're talking about not letting it define us as a person. For instance, it would be nice for people to comment on my writing this book, but do I *need* those comments to make me feel better about myself? Definitely not. If you like this book, great. If you don't like it, that's also great. It's part and parcel of the human experience. We can't be all things to all people.

It reminds me of a funny story Dr. Wayne Dyer told in one of his best-selling books. He phoned his wife to ask her where he was on the New York Times bestseller list. His wife said he wasn't anywhere on the list, but his book was at number two. Even the grandfather of self-help admitted that on very rare occasions, he fell into the trap of validation and approval.

If we *need* validation and approval from others, our life isn't our own. We're at the mercy of other people's opinions, constantly on our guard in case we get criticized. We become a sort of non-person, scared to take a stance or have an opinion on anything. People pleasing is our watchword, with all the downsides it brings. We constantly have to be seen as the nice guy/girl, lest we be judged harshly.

Unfortunately, we are living a delusion, No one judges us half as harshly as we are judging ourselves. Consider this: if we *need* validation and approval from others, it must follow we are people pleasers, and not in a good way. We have to suppress our wants and desires so as not to offend others. Let me give you an example.

If you knew a friend or relative was entering a televised singing competition and their voice sounded like fingernails on a blackboard, would you tell them?

I asked this exact question of someone I knew to be a people pleaser, and their reply was, "No, I wouldn't tell them in case they were offended." It didn't seem to matter that the would-be singing star was about to be humiliated on national television, as long as the people pleaser saved face and was seen as the nice guy/girl. What was *your* answer? What would you have done?

I would have suggested the singer book an appointment with a singing coach and ask them to give a professional and honest assessment of their ability. If they still went ahead despite what the professional said, they were also choosing to be humiliated, which of course was their prerogative, and they would have to be willing to pay the price for their fifteen minutes of fame. That's the downside of having free will.

Searching for happiness (Part 3)

When and how does people pleasing start? It starts around the time you become aware of rational thought. Someone praised us for doing something good, we liked the feeling, and before we knew it, we were looking to repeat the experience on a constant basis. Throw our education system and parents into the mix telling us we 'have to be nice' and shouldn't 'say no' and you have all the ingredients required to produce a people pleaser.

The main drawback for a people pleaser, which they see as a positive, is their chronic inability to have an opinion on anything. They have to be constantly dishonest. They will tell another person *exactly* what they think they want to hear, even when they're asked for an honest opinion. Never take one of these types to help you look at a used car you want to purchase. You will more than likely end up buying something that burns more oil than a power station. The person you take with you as a second pair of eyes will see the clouds of smoke, but they won't tell you, in case they offend. They don't mind you buying a pile of junk, as long as they don't offend. And yes, I have had this happen to me.

There's no need to go to the other extreme and become arrogant and opinionated, which is another form of insecurity. No, take the middle path of awareness. If you do, you'll be able to see exactly how much damage you're doing to your self-respect. Turn your awareness to your needs and wants once in a while. Focus on yourself for a change. Be aware the strategy you're employing is like giving pieces of yourself away. Sooner or later there won't be anything left to give away.

Some people are inclined to see kindness as weakness. Something to be exploited not applauded.

Wouldn't it be great if that wasn't so? Yes, it would, but unfortunately hoping doesn't make it so. You don't want a life where you constantly have to defer to others, unable to make any decisions of your own, worried in case you cause offense or displeasure, constantly on your guard to avoid even the slightest criticism, never becoming your own person. You don't want to be an extension of someone else, always pandering to how they feel.

We teach people every second of every day how they should treat us and where our boundaries are. If we don't respect ourselves should it come as a surprise we won't be respected by others?

Chasing success. What do your parents, the education system, advertising, the internet, other people and yourself have in common? They have contributed in different ways to molding, shaping and conditioning your version of what success 'should' look like. Work hard, study hard. Get a fantastic job, happy family, big car, big house and the big debt to go with it. If you acquire all these things, you're bound to be happy, right?

Are you happy? Has life lived up to the promises you were conditioned to believe it would? Or, like most people, do you believe something is missing? That one thing required to complete your life?

Unless you're sitting on a yacht somewhere in the Bahamas sipping cocktails, I very much doubt you're completely happy. Even if you *are* sitting on a yacht in the Bahamas, you may not be happy. You may have a nagging feeling that something's missing.

Worse still, even with all the trappings of success (however you define it), you're still not sure if you have enough or whether you might lose it all.

If we believe the tsunami of messages and advertising we are subjected to each day, most of us are losers in the game of life.

That is until you drop the *need* for success as a defining factor of your identity. We are constantly fed the impossible dream. *Obtain this, buy that, work hard and success will be yours for the taking.* All sounds so simple, doesn't it? And all with the subliminal message of 'if you're not all these things, you're a failure.'

Have you ever worked really hard at something? Really poured your heart and soul into it and it didn't work out? I certainly have. What was the overriding feeling you were left with? Probably failure, a feeling of being crushed and rejected. But why? The answer is simple; we have been fed a never-ending diet of *hard work equals success*. And if we fail, we didn't try hard enough.

In my experience, and probably yours too, hard work has only ever equaled hard work. Success only seems to happen if it's combined with talent and luck. Strange, isn't it, how these other variables never seem to get a mention in the quest for success. But if hard work always equals success, where are all the countless millions of successful people?

Don't get me wrong, I'm not advocating we shouldn't try. No, because that would be all or nothing thinking, and you already know how useless that is. What I *am* advocating is to not let success (or a lack thereof) define you as a person. A basic need to strive is encoded into our DNA; it's what's allowed us to evolve. And it worked beautifully thousands of years ago, but somehow the word 'success' seems to have slipped in under the radar. Success seems to have become the measure of us as a person rather than something we try to obtain. Is it any wonder we feel so bad when we don't achieve it?

By all means, become whatever you define as a success if that's what you need to do. But don't let success turn you into an arrogant, egotistical shadow of the person you once were. Become aware and understand that success like failure is only a concept you created. It isn't a commandment written in stone. You can change what *your* idea of being a success means to you at any time, and you don't have to accept a societal conditioned version of it.

Use your awareness and question why you need success. Don't blindly chase something without knowing why. I've seen this many times when working with sportsmen/sportswomen. They chase success in sport thinking it's the achievement they want when in fact they're compensating for some other form of insecurity in their lives. I know all too well how this feels as I did exactly the same.

Searching for happiness (Part 4)

I was trying and failing to fill the void depression was causing in my life with achieving sporting success, and I was relatively successful. The only problem was that I wasn't very happy. My unhappiness drove me to the point of obsession which in turn increased the experience of depression. A perfect vicious circle. The common theme amongst the sportsmen/sportswomen I worked with was 'I should be better.' Unfortunately, they'd fallen into the same trap I had. They believed hard work equals success.

If that were *truly* the case, they would have all been Olympic gold medalists. Sometimes we have to accept that no matter how hard we try we aren't going to get there if we don't have the necessary talent—plus a bit of luck. But our obsession with success, and the belief hard work is going to get us there, are responsible for a lot of dissatisfaction. Winning is great, but how you handle losing determines how far you get.

The act of chasing success ensures you never catch it. Your own psychology contrives to keep you feeling insecure and unfulfilled. It's the nature of your mind and your ego. Your ego doesn't understand the concept of *enough is enough*. It only understands *what's next*.

I saw a great example of this while watching an interview of someone who had won an Olympic gold medal. They said that once everyone had stopped congratulating them, they went back to their room in the Olympic village. They sat and looked at the medal in their hands and thought, *is this what I wasted four years of my life for? All the sacrifice and denial and for what?* That's the thing about success; it looks great from the outside. We don't get to see the anguish and sacrifice, only the end result.

By all means, strive to obtain the big house, the big car or the big bank account if it's what you think you need to complete you and make you appear successful. Don't define yourself as a failure if it doesn't turn out the way you envisaged because of some form of societal conditioning. Also, be aware that success requires sacrifice on the altar of contradiction. If you tell yourself 'family is everything,' how do you square that with having to work all hours of the day, thus ensuring you have no contact with your family? How do you square the acquisition of wealth with being too scared to spend it or worrying about losing it?

I want to share a story with you; it was written by Heinrich Böll in 1967. To me, the story exemplifies the difference between peace of mind and success and is called *The Fisherman and the Millionaire*.

An American investment banker was at the pier of a small coastal Mexican village when a small boat with one fisherman docked. Inside the small boat were several large yellowfins. The American complimented the Mexican on the quality of his fish and asked how long it took to catch them.

The Mexican replied, "Only a little while."

The American then asked why didn't he stay out longer and catch more fish?

The Mexican said he had enough to support his family's immediate needs.

The American then asked, "But what do you do with the rest of your time?"

The Mexican fisherman said, "I sleep late, fish a little, play with my children, take siestas with my wife, Maria, stroll into the village each evening where I sip wine, and play guitar with my amigos. I have a full and busy life."

The American scoffed, "I am a Harvard MBA and could help you. You should spend more time fishing and with the proceeds buy a bigger boat. With the proceeds from the bigger boat, you could buy several boats, and eventually, you would have a fleet of fishing boats. Instead of selling your catch to a middleman, you would sell directly to the processor, eventually opening your own cannery. You would control the product, processing, and distribution. You would need to leave this small coastal fishing village and move to Mexico City, then LA and eventually New York City, where you will run your expanding enterprise."

The Mexican fisherman asked, "But how long will this all take?"

To which the American replied, "Fifteen to twenty years."

"But what then?" asked the Mexican.

The American laughed and said, "That's the best part. When the time is right you would announce an IPO and sell your company stock to the public and become very rich, you would make millions!"

"Millions . . . then what?"

The American said, "Then you would retire. Move to a small coastal fishing village where you would sleep late, fish a little, play with your kids, take siestas with your wife, stroll to the village in the evenings where you could sip wine and play your guitar with your amigos."

I sincerely hope you understood the moral of that little story.

My story

I saved my personal story to the end because this book is about you, not me. My recovery from depression is actually quite boring and conventional. I have been on the therapy and medication route and will be eternally grateful for them both. However, there is something I did try differently that I want to share with you.

I've personally known and worked with quite a few people suffering from depression. One thing I've noticed (and it was the same for me) is a complete unwillingness to try anything which required commitment. A mental block to seeing something through—right to the very end—not with everyone, of course, but enough to make it noticeable. It's a common symptom of depression.

If you want to try the method I detail, you'll have to overcome this inertia and commit yourself totally for three months. Unfortunately, harsh as it may sound, there are no shortcuts, and no one can do it for you.

First and foremost, I have to tell you the depression I suffered for ten years was the reactive/situational type—I was reacting to my situation. If you suffer any other form of depression and want to try my method, by all means, do. Just monitor yourself closely. If the method starts to make you feel worse, maybe it's not for you.

As I was surfing the internet one day, I noticed an advertisement for using hypnotherapy to help with confidence building. As you already know, confidence is one of the first things you lose if you suffer depression. Although at the time I didn't have any preconceived opinions about the effectiveness or otherwise of hypnotherapy, I thought I'd give it a go. It was somewhat fortuitous I gave hypnosis a try, as it probably inspired me to become a hypnotherapist myself. Maybe some things are meant to happen.

Anyway, I downloaded the recordings for confidence, and listened to them twice a day for three months—in the mornings and before going to bed. I noticed something strange happening after the three months—the clouds of doom and gloom started to part slightly. I'm not talking about a choir of heavenly angels-type parting. No, just a slight gap, enough to allow a bit of hope to shine through. I actually felt a little more confident.

Now came the hard bit. I used the little bit of confidence I gained to engage in activities I hadn't done for years. Nothing dramatic, socializing a bit more and calling some friends I'd lost contact with over the years. I kept things small to make sure I wasn't overwhelmed so I could gain some traction. I worked at this for a further six months on a daily basis, and forced myself out of the house, back into some semblance of life.

My story (Part 2)

Guess what? It worked. Was it easy? No, it wasn't. It was difficult, but not impossible. There were plenty of times when I could have easily given up. But the thought of another ten years of suffering drove me on. And that's the attitude you'll need if you commit to my method. You will have to resist the urge to dismiss what I did because you think it's too simple and won't work for you. You will also have to resist the urge to think my method is a cure for depression because it isn't.

It's a way of facilitating a break in the clouds to transpire. The rest will be up to you and hopefully a competent therapist.

Someone a lot wiser than me once told me I would get out of depression the same way I got into it—on my own. As much as I hated to admit it, they were correct. Certainly, some people can lend a helping hand, but ultimately, it's down to us. When I look back at my depression, I now realize I was waiting for something to happen to take it away. I think I was waiting to be saved. I probably thought when I reached rock bottom everything would change. There was no rock bottom, only more of the same, so I was waiting for something which was never going to appear.

Hearing the constant repetition of confidence-giving messages caused a shift in my thought patterns—just enough to let a little bit of light peer through the gloom. I listened to those recordings long after I had my depression under control. By then I was a hypnotherapist myself and had learned there was nothing in those recordings which could remotely be thought of as a cure.

But, there was *something* that helped, and for this, I will always be grateful. There was something that helped me gain confidence, and apparently, it was the right thing at the right time.

Would I recommend one-on-one sessions with a hypnotherapist to help you through depression? Yes, I would if they were highly trained and qualified and used their skills alongside well-established therapy techniques. As with anything, do your research as there are a lot of people out there who can do you more harm than good. Get an iron-clad recommendation if you can. Don't make the mistake of thinking just because they're expensive they must be good. If you can find a certified therapist that also incorporates hypnosis, even better.

I hope you try my method, and it works fantastically well for you. Even if the method only helps you feel ten percent better, maybe the rest of the book will push you the other ninety percent or trigger you into finally reaching out for the help you deserve. The important thing is to take the first small step.

Final Thoughts

Well, folks! Here we are at the end of the book already and I sincerely hope it has been of value to you. I also hope you enjoyed reading it as much as I did writing it. If you take anything away from this book, please understand you are not alone in your battle with depression.

The illness can make us feel we are the only person in the world suffering, and nobody is in as much pain as we are. That's simply not true, although it can certainly feel like that at times. I have been where you are. I know exactly how demoralizing and hopeless it can feel at times, but you can overcome this. Depression wants you to stay stuck, apathetic and not caring about anything—it's the nature of the illness. Be proud of yourself that you took the first step out of this mire by buying this book. You are now being proactive with your illness instead of becoming a victim of it.

Keep that word *proactive* at the front and center of your mind. It needs to become your anchor as you journey through depression. If at times you feel overwhelmed and haven't the energy or the motivation to do anything consider picking up this book and opening it at any chapter. Make yourself a cup of coffee and commit to reading for ten minutes. It might just be enough to ignite your motivation and get you moving again, and the cherry on the cake is you are being proactive, even when you don't feel like it.

Always remember depression is an illness and not as some people believe a lifestyle choice or a way of gaining attention. Globally, more than 350 million people of all ages suffer from depression according to the World Health Organization. Statistically, a quarter of the world's population will have a depressive episode at least once in their lives. That's an awful lot of people suffering in silence.

Knowledge is power. I hope I have imparted some knowledge that will inspire you to take your power back and not suffer in silence by getting the help you need and deserve. Remember being proactive is the key to recovery from depression. Make reading a chapter a day part of your routine. All that remains is for me to thank you for buying my book and to wish you a speedy recovery. Till next time. Good luck.

If you have been affected in any way by reading this book and feel the need to talk to someone, I have included some helpline numbers on the next page.

Helpline Numbers

Need help? Contact a suicide hotline if you need someone to talk to. If you have a friend in need of help, please encourage that person to contact a suicide hotline as well.

- Worldwide
In general, if you're outside the US, numbers for your country are here: Help a friend - Befrienders Worldwide. You can also e-mail jo@samaritans.org to talk to someone or go to http://www.samaritans.org/how-we . . . to speak with someone.

- United States
Call the **National Suicide Prevention Lifeline** at 1-800-273-TALK (8255)

Para español, llame al 1-888-628-9454.

- Canada
Locate a crisis center in your area and at The Canadian Association for Suicide Prevention (link to: **https://suicideprevention.ca/nee** . . .). For youth under 20, you can call the Kids Help Phone at 1-800-668-6868.

- India
Visit **AASRA** or call their 24/7 helpline at +91-22-27546669 or +91-22-27546667. You can also e-mail aasrahelpline@yahoo.com.

- UK 116 123 (to reach the Samaritans in the UK)

- France (33) 01 46 21 46 46

- Australia 13 11 14

Disclaimer

Grahame Cossum makes no claims that the information he provides is always completely accurate and up-to-date, and readers must check primary sources before relying on such information or opinion. Under no circumstances should the material contained in the book be used as a replacement for therapeutic intervention as it is intended for information purposes only. Any persons' names contained in the book are completely fictitious. Any stories are heavily blurred to ensure confidentiality.

Printed in Great Britain
by Amazon